UTAH
REFLECTIONS

UTAH REFLECTIONS

Stories from the Wasatch Front

EDITED BY
Sherri H. Hoffman, Kase Johnstun & Mary Johnstun

Published by The History Press
Charleston, SC 29403
www.historypress.net

Copyright © 2014 by Sherri H. Hoffman, Kase Johnstun and Mary Johnstun
All rights reserved

"The Pit Bull and the Mountain Goat" from *A Little More About Me* by Pam Houston. Copyright © 1999 by Pam Houston. Used by permission of W.W. Norton & Company, Inc.
"Bald Eagles," excerpt(s) from *Refuge: An Unnatural History of Family and Place* by Terry Tempest Williams, copyright © 1991 by Terry Tempest Williams. Used by permission of Pantheon Books, an imprint of the Knopf Doubleday Publishing Group, a division of Random House LLC. All rights reserved.
"Looking for *Spiral Jetty*" by Lance Larsen was the winner of the Writers at Work Nonfiction Prize and originally appeared in *Quarterly West.*
"February 14" by Katharine Coles was originally published in *Narrative.*
Portions of "The Curling Fingers of the Hatch Women" by Jana Richman were originally printed in her biography *Riding in the Shadow of Saints* (Random House, 2006).

Cover photo credits to Jason Chacon, Dane Webster and Jen Henderson.
Lynn Kilpatrick's author photo credit to Zoe Rodriguez (www.zoerodriguez.me/index.html).
Terry Tempest Williams's author photo credit to Marion Ettlinger.

First published 2014

ISBN 978-1-5402-2299-2

Library of Congress CIP data applied for.

Notice: The information in this book is true and complete to the best of our knowledge. It is offered without guarantee on the part of the author or The History Press. The author and The History Press disclaim all liability in connection with the use of this book.

All rights reserved. No part of this book may be reproduced or transmitted in any form whatsoever without prior written permission from the publisher except in the case of brief quotations embodied in critical articles and reviews.

CONTENTS

Acknowledgements	7
Introduction, by Sherri H. Hoffman	9
1. Bounty, by Phyllis Barber	13
2. Looking for *Spiral Jetty*, by Lance Larsen	20
3. The Garden, by James R. West	33
4. The Pit Bull and the Mountain Goat, by Pam Houston	41
5. The Curling Fingers of the Hatch Women, by Jana Richman	52
6. The Prayer Hole, by J. Scott Hale	59
7. Bald Eagles, by Terry Tempest Williams	62
8. February 14, by Katharine Coles	69
9. The Wasatch Front and Back, by Stevan Allred	71
10. Geographies of Home, by Jen Henderson	77
11. Evaporation, by Sylvia Torti	84
12. Finding the Slow Lane, by Joni Haws	90
13. Some Lines on Faults: An Insomniac's Diary, by Lynn Kilpatrick	97
14. Hold This, by Kase Johnstun	103
15. Intimations of Vitality: Climbing Little Cottonwood, by Jeffrey McCarthy	107
16. Then Came November, by Chadd VanZanten	111
About the Authors	119
About the Editors	125

ACKNOWLEDGEMENTS

We would like to thank all the authors who contributed their hearts in the form of narratives and their photos that truly capture what it means to be a part of living in the Wasatch Front and Cache Valley.

We would like to thank Will McKay for his guidance and patience throughout and The History Press for its recognizing the value that this anthology brings to not only the literary world but also the people of the Wasatch Front and, hopefully, the many classrooms that could benefit from a collection of regional essays such as these.

Sherri would like to thank her husband, Rick, and her mother and father, DeVon and Dianne Hale, for all their support and guidance throughout.

Mary and Kase would like to thank Sherri for her hard work and dedication to this project and Lukas Diego for being a big kid and showing his mom and dad all the wonderful reasons to raise their boy along the Wasatch Front.

INTRODUCTION

I was born in the Salt Lake Valley at the Catholic hospital, Holy Cross. My parents were recent graduates from the University of Utah, and my dad was just starting medical school. To this day, they'll point out the basement apartment with windows that peek up along the foundation of the Second Avenue house where they took me as an infant from the hospital and snuggled me into a bureau drawer that served as a bassinet. Along the east bench near where they live now, the air shifts with the seasons, summer heat and winter cold, and on your tongue, the salt of black-flecked rock, scrub oak, sage and dry grass and spring rains that carry the smell of faraway snow.

At night, the streets glitter in a geometric grid hung with yellow lights, the boxy demarcation of commerce, schools and neighborhoods. The bright center of the city is the Mormon temple, a massive angular construct of granite with six spires, an angel mounted to the uppermost point, facing east, mouth affixed to a golden trumpet. When I was a little girl, my father told me the angel was Harry James, the famous jazz trumpeter from the big band era. Of course, I knew the Mormon angel was called Moroni, herald to the second coming of their Savior, but I wanted to believe it was about the music. From the east bench, the golden angel marks the nexus of the valley—dark, abrupt mountains of the Wasatch Front to the east, Great Salt Lake to the west—and the valley itself evokes both a density of populace and a vastness of open space.

That's the paradox of the Wasatch Front—what it contains alongside that which it cannot contain. Granite peaks rise from the distinct shelf cut

Introduction

Wellsville mountains above the Cache Valley. *Photo credit Danel W. Bachman.*

by the prehistoric pluvial lake where seashells and fossilized sea creatures can still be found above 4,500 feet. Glacial-carved canyons open onto wide city blocks inhabited by architectural monuments built of local stone and buildings from which at any time you may spot urbanized mule deer, coyotes, water fowl or raptors or an occasional moose. The local industries boast master craftsmen, research and technology, mining, farming and water management in this high-mountain desert. The mountain peaks are capped with snow envied worldwide, and to the west is the largest saltwater lake in the Western Hemisphere.

The essays, stories and poetry collected here embrace the paradox of this place. It is the home to which we return and the home we never left. A bounty rich with traditions and sustenance, physically and spiritually. A geographic anomaly of minerals, earth, rock and elements settled by folks seeking the common aspirations of every people—a roof over their heads, a plot of land, space to raise up children and the freedom to worship as they believe. It is a place of wilderness and amenity. Of harsh weather and ebullient outdoor sports. Of rock and water. Salt and faith.

The geographic journey extends far beyond the old highways that ride the shoulders of the Front, past the lakefronts and the climbing

INTRODUCTION

canyons—Provo, Ogden, Logan, Big or Little Cottonwood, Millcreek or Emigration. When I was a teenager, my family lived in southern Idaho, and on every car trip to and from my Uncle John's dairy farm in Benson, Utah, my father identified the alluvial gap in Red Rock Pass that released the ancient Lake Bonneville into the Snake River system, flooding what is now the Columbia Gorge in the Pacific Northwest. That gap remains a familial marker, the gateway into the fabulous world of my uncle's farm where our grown-up cousins would take us to the banks of the Bear River on ATVs, haul us in the tractors as they fed the herds of ponderous Holsteins and enlist our clumsy skills to bottle-feed the bawling calves.

The Wasatch Front is resplendent with those geographic touchstones that coalesce into memory: fruit stands and drive-ins, vegetable gardens, cherry orchards and the heart-stopping white wood-frame roller coaster at Lagoon. Old pathways return us to places of our childhoods, families and the reminiscent fullness of the Wasatch Front as renewal or memorial. Or discovery. I'll admit, in all the years I lived in Utah as an adult—through college and a first marriage—I'd never heard of the massive art installation in the lake near Rozel Point, less than forty miles as the crow flies from the home in Roy where I grew my own vegetables and fruit in the backyard. I knew no art installation, but my garden was as commonplace as a front door—everyone had one. Even if the structures are different, the *principles* are the same.

If there's anything that Utah has more of than gardens *or* front doors, it's principles. Religious freedom attracted the original Mormon pioneers, and they considered family histories so essential that the culture continues to embrace the genealogical process both forward and back in time. More recently but still years before the "Greatest Snow on Earth" secured the installment of Olympic Park and the 2002 Olympic events in Deer Valley and Park City, the locals have been skiing the coveted powder on the likes of Sugarloaf and Bald Mountain with worshipful abandon. Then with every turning of the seasons, the snowmelt feeds the streams and rivers that reach to Great Salt Lake with all the miraculous sanctity of water in a desert. And if you leapt across the mountain tops from Jupiter Peak to Mount Timpanogos, across the Utah Valley to Flat Top in the Oquirrh Mountains, you'd be in the Bingham Canyon Mine, the largest open pit mine in the world, principled in venture and commerce.

Any history of the Wasatch Front is not without hardship, for it remains a wilderness replete with challenges of scarcity, environment, human suffering, love and loss. Many of the original settlers arrived in ox carts or on

Introduction

Mount Timpanogos sits over the valley like a giant. *Photo credit Mike Jensen.*

foot, pulling handcarts from the East and singing walking songs: "For some must push and some must pull as we go marching up the hill. So merrily on our way we go, until we reach the Valley-Oh!" Pushed and pulled, these pioneers may have graced the Wasatch Front with an indomitable spirit of optimism, embracing the fundamental connections to this unique land in a way that makes life and the measure of life sacred. This is the push and pull that returns us to the Wasatch Front, time and again, even if it is only in our hearts. So vast and deep are its effects that these mountains, these waterways, these lakes, these rocks and trees—all of what the Wasatch Front is and ever has been—remain with each of us who ever remembers calling this place home, perhaps even generationally. We carry our memories into the world, collected like so much water in a geographic basin, a reminder and a confirmation of a foundational presence that is at once constant and ever-changing, seasonal and ceaseless, and endowed with an essential fullness of hope.

—Sherri H. Hoffman

Chapter 1

BOUNTY

by Phyllis Barber

"So, what is the Wasatch Front exactly?" I ask my sister, Kathy. I'm driving. We're headed north on I-15 on a golden-haze-of-a-day in October. The wall of the Wasatch Range rises on the right side of the car. The peaks of Ben Lomond and Mount Ogden block out a huge chunk of eastern sky. "What is the extent of it, like how many miles long?"

"I think it's the urban areas," she says. "Provo, Salt Lake, Ogden." Then she checks her iPhone, which knows everything, though the truth is that Kathy is a genuine repository of facts and information, even without her phone. I listen to the tires of my car turning on asphalt while she presses keys and slides screens. I think about harvest time and how our mother's Idaho farmer genes have propelled us northward once again.

"'The Wasatch Front consists of a chain of some twenty-five cities,'" she reads out loud, "'stretched along the Wasatch Range from approximately Santaquin in the south to Brigham City in the north.'" There is real surprise in her voice. "It's longer than I thought. One hundred sixty miles from the Utah-Idaho border through central Utah."

"I'm glad to hear it's that long," I say.

We are headed to Willard, Utah, and, for reasons I can't explain, I want that small, side-of-the-road town in northern Utah to be part of the Wasatch Front. I want the Front to include the rural as well as the urban. A habitual, even perverse, dissector of words and definitions, I'm resisting the idea of the Wasatch Front as a chain of cities, which seems to be an impossibly narrow focus on human populations. I want the Front to be more than Provo, Salt Lake and Ogden. More than cities themselves.

Utah Reflections

25th Street in Ogden. *Art credit Leah Webb Palmer.*

Granted, I'm making my own semantic mountains out of molehills, but the definition Kathy read mentions the Wasatch Range almost as an afterthought. How can anyone even think about the Wasatch Front without first considering the Range that dwarfs these cities? Without those mountains that rise and stretch as if to Alaska if we wanted to go that far (it's that kind of day), though the interstate probably loses itself at the Canadian border, and we are only going to Willard? How could you not focus on the incomprehensible wall of mountains where these cities are nestled when you say "the Wasatch Front?" The mountains that tower and wrinkle and fold and feel like the arms of a great protector, sometimes menacing, sometimes beneficent? The great mass that lifts out of the desert, out of the Great Basin that can be desolate and unforgiving with its many square miles of sand, desolate salt flats, proving grounds (whatever those are trying to prove), buried munitions and test and training ranges—in other words, no man's land?

The solid, sometimes scrub-oak green, sometimes evergreen, sometimes brown and rust colors of autumn or sometimes snow-white Wasatch Mountains have a presence like no other, even though I've visited Machu Picchu and the Himalayas and the many other high places in the world and offer my most humble praise to their presence. My relationship with the Wasatch Range, however, is an intimate, personal one. Words like "eternal," "everlasting," "a mighty fortress," words from hymns I learned as a child, come to mind when looking at these mountains. I am in awe. They are not something anyone can capture in words, though sometimes I try with paltry jabs into the jungle of language—the sound of a child pounding on an upside-down kettle with a wooden spoon—sky temples, power personified, guardians, bold, brash, mighty, seductive, brutal, intriguing, stellar, magnificent, awesome, majestic…which sentence goes to show you that no words can cover the terrain of what it means when you say "Wasatch Front." The mountains themselves are the over-the-top creators of speechlessness. Definable or not, they bring out a primal urge to love, adore, fear, worship, respect and praise. That's what mountains are all about in my book.

As a child, driving with our family to Idaho from southern Nevada every summer, I was always fascinated by the appearance of the twelve-thousand-foot Mount Nebo, the beginning of the Wasatch Range. Stark. Bold. This eons-ago eruption/tumultuous uplift suddenly in full view, making me feel that we were traveling inside a creeping insect rather than a motorcar. Then, as a student at Brigham Young University in the '60s, I often stopped after a tiring day of classes to marvel at the purple-orange sunset reflected off the face of the snow-covered Mount Timpanogos—a mountain of majesty if there ever was one. I felt more secure, more solid and less lonely as I gazed at its everlasting hills. Later, living in Salt Lake City for twenty years, raising children and waking to a picture window full of the grandiose Mount Olympus every day, that piece of the Wasatch Front imprinted itself in my memory, most likely forever, or at least until I catch the last ounce of air in my lungs. The whole family was inspired by being able to look up at these mountains, humble pilgrims reminded daily that there is always a mountain to climb and always something much larger than ourselves. I will never forget Mount Olympus and Lone Peak wrapped in clouds, spotted with shadows, their winter majesty and springtime velvety green rising up and up toward the sky and making small things seem much more possible. These mountains stood so huge outside our window that it inspired mythological thoughts of Prometheus, Oden and Zeus, especially when topped with a ring of leaden clouds. The Wasatch Range: a mighty fortress, a wall, a barrier to desert winds, the east edge of the Great Basin, that 225,000-square-mile sink in the desert.

Kathy and I were born in the south end of that sink. In the Mojave Desert. The uplifted southern end of that Great Basin. In Boulder City and

Las Vegas, Nevada. And today, Kathy and I are driving along the edge of the bowl of the Great Basin, traversing one of the bathtub rings of the ancient Bonneville Lake that once covered Utah, Nevada, parts of Idaho and Oregon. Skimming north with the imposing Wasatch Range at our side, we're looking for the weathered billboard that announces "Utah's Famous Fruit Way," the turnoff to Highway 89.

Which leads me to my second thought about the Wasatch Front. I love what happens at the foot of these mountains—in the foothills, on the fertile land, among the people who have survived and thrived since the Mormon pioneers arrived in 1847, the people who farm and till and make the valley blossom like a rose; who sing and dance; who take the light rail to the Jazz, Bee's, Real Salt Lake games; who listen to heavy metal, country and the Tabernacle Choir; who perform the living that happens here. The down-to-earth essence of the Wasatch Front to me, besides the mountains themselves, would be the fruit stands found on both the south and north ends of the Front. They are an integral part of the Wasatch Front, if not, to my way of thinking, the essential Wasatch Front.

And today we're headed for the foothills of Willard Peak, to Perry City and Willard, the towns with an inheritance of orchards that overlook the Great Salt Lake, the briny remnant of Lake Bonneville that sat heavy in the Great Basin for thousands of years before draining off and evaporating. The fruit stands are at the fertile heart of the Wasatch Front, definitely one of its finest features and one of the tangible results of Brigham Young's first pronouncement when he stood tall in the back of the wagon before collapsing into a feverish state once again (too many days on the trail): "This is The Place."

We've been here before. Many times. When Kathy and I were children, on our annual trek to Idaho to visit our mother's family, Dad would pull over to a variety of fruit stands—for cherries and apricots in July, for peaches and pears and plums if we traveled later in the summer. Even though today we maintain ourselves as sophisticated Park City girls, we come from a humble family tree populated by Danish and Mormon pioneers, most of whom were farmers. We're reenacting the ritual of our yearly family car rides from southern Nevada to Idaho—our subliminal attempt to own the harvest. There's still magic for us in those fruit stands with their assortment of honeys, jams and jellies; the colorful array of local peppers—Kung Pao, Serrano, Habañero, Anaheim, Sweet Banana; the possibility of making a pumpkin pie from scratch; and an excuse to purchase a handmade caramel, dietary caution to the wind.

Phyllis Barber stands with her sister Kathy Gold, holding the day's purchases. *Photo credit Phyllis Barber.*

Once a year, a giant metaphor of a fishing pole reaches out over the Wasatch Mountains into the Wasatch Back where we live and catches us with its bait. We can't help but take a bite. My car almost runs under its own volition—out the driveway, over to Kathy's house—heading for the I-15 corridor, heading for fresh pears at their peak, the fuzz of a new peach, the Radio Flyer wagons full of pumpkins and the stands stacked with the bounties of the squash crop: Blue Hubbards, Butternuts, Bananas, Spaghettis, Festivals, Buckskins, Brittlenuts, Turk Turbans and Acorns.

"There it is," Kathy says when she spots the faded, weather-battered sign. "I wonder how old it is?"

"Utah's Famous Fruit Way," it reads. Willard and Perry, Utah. Highway 89. Next exit.

Willard, by the way, was home to our great-great-grandfather James Willard Hubbard, who married a Pettingill, which is the name above the first side-of-the-road fruit stand we find after turning off the freeway. "Pettingill Produce," a thriving fruit stand with only one or two skinny parking spots available at this hour. I squeeze my car into a place next to the homemade metal statue of a giant peach, five feet across, somewhat worse for wear but still *the* giant peach—forget about James and his Giant Peach.

I cut the engine. We jump out of the car, no slow unfolding here. We're in a wonderland: bins of apples—Cameo, Braeburn, Fuji, Red Delicious. Yes. Boxes and crates full of Bartlett pears. Yes. The salesperson cuts us a juicy wedge to taste. Yes. Yes. We walk past piles of cornstalks and straw people and a sign that says, "Wagon rides today at 11 and 4. All Ages." Maybe no to that one, as we have miles to go before we sleep. A row of pumpkins have been drilled with holes in the style of Mexican luminarias.

Then, an amateurish mural catches my attention. Two painted pirates, with round, vacant cutout holes for heads, wear tri-cornered hats and yellow-painted buttons on their red and blue coats. A skull-and-crossbones flag flaps on a mast in the background. A three-step stool has been placed behind this painting-on-wood, and two children have climbed up behind the mural to poke their heads through the holes while their parents take pictures. Mutiny on the Bounty. Buccaneers. Swashbucklers, ahoy. What with all this booty around here, it's tempting, for one fanciful moment, to think *Shiver me timbers, matey*, to imagine a pirate ship at the ready at a Willard Bay dock. Except the Great Salt Lake has no rivers to follow to new places, a land-bound sea, no place to freight our produce, even if we wanted to capture all this cargo.

Bounty. Harvest. Bountiful: marked by abundance; plentiful. Golden haze on the meadow behind Pettingill's where the spent peach trees have given up their fruit. Their leaves are saying goodbye for this year—green on the treetops, yellow in the middle and bright orange at the base of their branches. It's autumn. Water sparkles on the beautiful blue Willard Bay that stretches out beyond the quiltwork of harvested fields, barns and horse sheds between Highway 89 and I-15. In someone's fields, water sprays quietly from the spindly arms of a rolling irrigation system. A herd of elk grazes in open fields, blissful in the thick grass between the gnarled tree trunks in the orchards. Pastoral. Picturesque.

Something about home here. Something about stability and solidity, this land, these trees that bear fruit, these people who grow food and work the soil. Something in the blood about being a farmer. Something about planting seeds and harvesting the results.

Next stop: Roy's Fruit Stand. Self-service. A camouflage net hangs over a beleaguered set of shelves covered with a limp green tarp. A few pumpkins and some misshapen squash have been left to fend for themselves, fifty cents apiece. Roy seems to have been the creator of sci-fi squash: pod people with grayish green skins that protect the unsold produce from would-be kleptos. But the stand is too isolated. Too abandoned. The idea of no one home is not appealing to us, even for fifty cents a shot and a pod squash. We like to talk to the people who run these stands. We drive on to Grammy's Fruit N Produce and search for another parking place.

"Please for your safety, do not climb on the pumpkin piles," one sign says. "Please don't crawl on me or pick me up by my stem. You'll mess up my good looks," another one says. "Onions, $6 a bag." "Sweet Spanish. Twenty-five pounds." And Grammy's has the most complete array of peppers we've seen yet, including the infamous Ghost Chili, the world's hottest pepper. The salesgirl looks healthy enough, even though she boasts of having eaten the Ghost Chili three times. She verifies that it is, indeed, the world's hottest. It is a hot never to be forgotten among humankind, she implies. And rather than take her on by conducting our own test, we admire instead the many colors and varieties of chilis at Grammy's. So many gifts from nature and from the land and from the foothills of the Wasatch Front.

From Grammy's, the view of the fields between us and the water itself is spectacular today, the sun doing its sparkle thing on the immense expanse of light blue. Behind Grammy's, the peach trees in the almost fallow orchards are exhibitionists extraordinaire—a jumble of green, yellow and the haunting color of pumpkins and squash. Autumn everywhere.

"This satisfies something in me," Kathy says as we load the car trunk full of our packages, bags and hopeful visions of piping-hot fruit cobbler, pear compote, applesauce, maybe even apple cider. "Something about this touches a primitive instinct I feel but can't articulate."

"We're hunting and gathering," I joke, then respond to something inside of me that's inviting me to a moment of quiet. What more can I say? I can't talk about what I'm feeling either. It's deep in there somewhere but not fetchable at the moment.

We drive to Maddox for its Famous Fried Chicken. It is also the place where "4,000 head of choice beef are used annually for people who care about excellence." That's a lot of choice beef meeting the end of their days, but the food tastes better because we are at the drive-in part of the restaurant where we can watch people in Dodge Rams, Silverados, minivans and cowboy hats ordering lunch for their children and themselves. We are watching the farmers, the ranchers, the cowboys and those who would keep the world fed pause in the middle of the day to feed themselves. We succumb to an order of the famous chicken and to one of the burgers made from excellence. We sigh over the root beer floats. We are blissed out.

"Something about this…" Kathy says again.

Maybe the words will never be enough, but it doesn't matter. We are bounty hunters on the Wasatch Front. We are big-little girls revisiting smells and tastes from our childhood. Our parents are walking behind us, carrying paper bags to the car. They are tucking the produce in the trunk where it won't get bruised. They are saving a peach for each child and searching for napkins. Our parents are feeding us. They, and we in their stead, are taking our part in the eternal harvest, the change of seasons, the hunting, the gathering, the nourishing, the turn of the wheel.

Chapter 2

LOOKING FOR SPIRAL JETTY

by Lance Larsen

1.

I first came across Robert Smithson's *Spiral Jetty* (1970), as most people do, in an art history book. There it was, 15 feet wide, 1,600 feet long—a giant stone-and-gravel earthwork coiled in on itself, lying in a lake, a frozen vortex. Though I was a little suspicious—wasn't art supposed to hang in museums?—something about it intrigued me. Its scale for one thing, not to mention Smithson's audacity. What's more, it seemed old from the moment it was created, almost as if the Great Salt Lake had been brooding over a favorite archetype for aeons and had just recently allowed it to hatch and surface. This was in the early 1980s. During the next twenty years, whenever I flew into or out of the Salt Lake Airport, I always scanned the water from the plane. Never mind that the jetty was completely submerged and had been since 1972. Never mind that I was searching the wrong end of the lake. I believed if I zenned myself into tranquility and willed the lake into cooperation, I might get lucky and glimpse the jetty. Maybe it really was the gigantic snake it resembled and, under the cover of water, moved at will. I saw nothing. But seeing nothing, I thought of Atlantis. Which left me sad and exhilarated and wanting to believe in mystery.

The *Spiral Jetty*. Photo credit Mike Harshman.

2.

Spiral Jetty is commonly referred to as the most infrequently seen major contemporary artwork in the world. Recently, broad prevailing climatic patterns conspired to change that. By the fall of 2002, after five years of Utah drought, the Great Salt Lake was at its lowest level in thirty years. And *Spiral Jetty* was once again visible. After a friend's rhapsodic recommendation, I decided to see for myself. I had on my side a delicious Saturday in October and a short two-hour drive from my home. I had a map and detailed directions pulled off the Internet. I had my artist wife, Jacqui, to serve as guide and our two children, Derek (twelve) and Brooke (nine), to provide color and commentary. I had the devotee's sense of pilgrimage, the adventurer's sense of wanderlust and let-happen-what-will-happen.

3.

Between the third and fourth drafts of this essay, I grew weary of italicizing *Spiral Jetty*. It was more than the inconvenience of reaching over to click the mouse. Italics seemed to lie or at least distort. Certainly *Spiral Jetty* was art, but increasingly Spiral Jetty was place, and at times spiral jetty felt like land form. I can see my quandariness taking me far afield into abbreviation, pet names, neologism, so I have made a pact with myself: to be of three minds only. Sometimes ambivalence marks affection.

4.

I drive I-15 regularly and manage, during most trips, to ignore what I see. But this trip, with Spiral Jetty as destination, even the most mundane objects stood out, multiplied for once by their secret life as art. A cheaply made white brick church: worship inside a nautilus. An inflated stegosaurus overseeing an end-of-month used-car blitzkrieg: mysteries of the past. A labyrinthine corn maze: a manifestation of the collective unconscious. Even the freight train heading south, graffitied with illegible ballooned-up names, seemed apropos. Here was the work of a graffiti artist or lonely hearts poet, who, like Smithson, intuited the pull of the conceptual: sending a piece of oneself on tour, entering hundreds of cities on the sly, interrupting a dazed field hand outside Abilene or an underage couple necking at a railroad crossing in Peoria. It was as if Spiral Jetty were magnetic north, causing everything in its wake to vibrate with newly charged ions.

5.

jetty \je-te\ n, pl **jetties**.—n. **1**: a structure of stones, piles, or the like, projecting into the sea or other body of water to protect a harbor, deflect the current etc. **2**: a wharf or landing pier. **3**: a protecting frame of a pier. **4**: a part of a building that projects beyond the rest. **5**: a protecting outwork: bastion, bulwark. [1375–1425; late ME *get(t)ey* < OF *jetee*, lit., something thrown out, a projection, to throw]

6.

Just past the halfway mark to Spiral Jetty, Jacqui pointed out the window: "See the B?" Half a mile away, a white concrete letter seventy feet high emblazoned the foothills of the Wasatch Front. I suppose westerners began this tradition of placing initials above their settlements out of pride. Pride for a town or a high school—in this case Bountiful, which the highway mercifully skirted. "When Lee Biggs was in his seventies, he used to walk up there every morning," Jacqui said. Lee Biggs was her grandfather. She always called him by both names—a formality that made him more skinny and cantankerous and down-home wise, especially now that he was dead six years.

"He'd walk up to the B, then over to the V," Jacqui said. "Three miles in all."

It took me a while to find the V. "What's the V for? Some school mascot—Vandals, Varmints, Vagrants?"

"No idea," Jacqui said. The letters were ludicrous and charming and grew more so the longer you looked at them. Perhaps the chamber of commerce wanted to extend an invitation to very high-flying, very literate Canada geese. Or lay down verbal clues against a case of collective amnesia sweeping the town, rendering everyone forgetful of where they lived. What would these letters have meant to Lee Biggs? Their prominence was not unlike a beautifully useless jetty on a saline lake. The difference: Lee Biggs and thirty-seven thousand Bountifulites knew what B and V stood for. The difference: few observers would call the B and V sublime.

The *Spiral Jetty*. Photo credit Ron Toole.

7.

Jacqui read aloud a Smithson essay she'd brought along. His work in 1968 with salt lakes in California, spurred by interest in Bolivian saline lakes stained red by micro bacteria, led him eventually to Rozel Point, on the north end of Great Salt Lake, where he discovered water "the color of tomato soup." Here, on a shoreline dotted with industrial debris and machinery left over from attempts to extract oil from the lake, he had a vision of sorts:

> *As I looked at the site, it reverberated out to the horizons only to suggest an immobile cyclone while flickering light made the entire landscape appear to quake. A dormant earthquake spread into the fluttering stillness, into a spinning sensation without movement. This site was a rotary that enclosed itself in an immense roundness. From that gyrating space emerged the possibility of the Spiral Jetty.*

This passage was followed by patches of extraordinary purple prose. Yes, Smithson was illuminating, chancy, richly suggestive, but also abstract. Abstract and overreaching—at least in his language. Our drive north became a study in contrasts. Outside the car, a predictable suburban landscape of tract housing, trailer parks, strip malls. Inside, a torrent of descriptions so dense and bizarre, so torqued with technical and hallucinogenic language that I felt I was inside one of those fast-food salad containers that has been violently shaken until every sentence drips with too much dressing.

8.

Perhaps I'm just as guilty as Smithson. Two days before our trip, I found myself trying to explain Ihab Hassan's "Toward a Concept of Postmodernism" to sleepy English majors. One student was completely baffled. "Okay," I said, "let's try an example." I wrote Robert Smithson's name on the board. "Anyone heard of him?" No one raised a hand. "How about *Spiral Jetty?*" Three hands went up. "An earth work created in 1970," I said, "in the Great Salt Lake," then I sketched in relevant background. On the blackboard I rendered *Spiral Jetty* the best I could—a bass clef with a bad case of inner turmoil. I mentioned Cristo and his two-and-a-half-mile fabric fence in Marin County and Walter de Maria's New Mexico field filled with lightning rods. Then I launched into a series of questions. "How is this piece different from a painting? Where does its meaning inhere—in conceptual framework or execution? In putting together enough funding to move several tons of the earth's surface from one location to another? In Smithson running along it and looking up at a helicopter? In the black-and-white photo that graces dozens of art history books? In being underwater for thirty years, then reappearing? In aficionados flying in from all over the world to view it, as they've been doing in great numbers this fall? In a professor like me asking questions he can't answer about a piece of art he's never seen?"

9.

At Promontory, Utah, ten miles shy of Spiral Jetty, where the Union Pacific Railroad met the Central Pacific in 1869, where immigrants and former slaves put down their picks for thirty-five minutes so Leland Stanford could drive a golden spike, we stopped for a restroom break. Afterward, we approached the counter at the Visitors' Center.

"Can I help you?"

The park attendant, mid-forties, had the croakiest smoker's voice I'd ever heard.

"Yes," I said. "What can you tell me about Spiral Jetty?"

She reached for a photocopy of a *New York Times* piece from a few weeks before and handed it to me. "Now that it's reached *masterpiece status*"—she paused to make quotation marks in the air—"everyone wants to see it."

She went on to explain the impact since late August. Thousands of people pouring in from New York. Frantic long-distance calls asking which airport to fly into, though there's only one. Visitors getting run off the road. "Those New Yorkers waiting 'til November to book a flight are taking a chance. If we get an early snow, the county will just close down the road."

She looked hard at me. "You need to know there are no facilities down there, no fresh water. And the salt, it's dangerous. If you fall down, it cuts like broken glass."

It wasn't until this point in the conversation that she let slip that she herself hadn't seen *Spiral Jetty*.

"Really?" Jacqui said. "It's only ten miles away."

"Don't get me wrong," the attendant said. "I want to see it. And our supervisor, he's seen it. We might go as a staff at the end of the month."

10.

In the near-empty parking lot, I started up our Toyota van and then slowly drove the perimeter, in a giant circle, cranking the steering wheel a little more tightly to the left with each revolution. Derek and Brooke put their hands up and, leaning, did the wave. Finally, we came to a dead stop, as if we had located some cosmic epicenter and expected to be beamed up into a celestial pleasure bus.

"What was that about?" Jacqui said.

"Getting us in the mood."

11.

Immediately after Promontory, the road turned primitive. We navigated by cattle guard, fence line and broken corral. And because our car was originally from Canada, we multiplied dirt road and dead sunflowers and anthills by 0.61 to convert map miles into car kilometers. We dodged boulders, slid carefully over potholes and thanked the shaky hand that painted SPIRL

The *Spiral Jetty*. Photo credit Ben Steiner.

JETTY and an arrow to the right on a rotting piece of wood. Twenty-five minutes later, we parked beside an abandoned and preposterously pink mobile home, one side torn open. This, according to our directions, was the final landmark.

12.

"Was this in a war?" my daughter asked. She rubbed a cluster of bullet holes in the chassis of an amphibious vehicle the size of a tank. We'd pulled off to the side of the road, gathered our supplies into two backpacks for the walk down to the shore and locked the car. This vehicle and the spent carcass of a Dodge truck beside it resembled dinosaurs that might have pulled themselves from the saline muck and expired. I wanted to say, *Depends what you mean by war.*

"Probably not," I said. "Just someone taking target practice."

13.

"Where's the jetty?" This time it was my son. I hate it when he gives voice to my own questions. Here we were, but where was it? Between us and the lake, which he was dutifully scanning, lay a cornucopia of rusted machines and oil barrels, car parts, cable and, from a seepy hole beside the lake, a stench so rank Brooke plugged her nose. Directly in front of us lay a jetty—one used to transport drilling equipment—but no spiral to it, no curve at all. From the end of the jetty, and running parallel to the shore, a line of ancient timbers stuck up from the water. Smithson's perspective was dead on: shoreline as modern wasteland. Yet there was something beautiful in the bleakness, not unlike a post-nuclear landscape in an Andrei Tarkovsky film. You're trapped by the camera into slowing down. And in slowing down, you go inside yourself.

14.

We picked our way along the shore, everything masquerading as what it wasn't. Dirty sand: salt. Snowdrifts that have melted and re-frozen: salt. Patchy pieces of ice: more salt. The dirt in the snowdrifts: millions of dead flies. A broken kite: a dead pelican. A kid's matchbox car striped yellow: a decomposing Jerusalem cricket. My son lifted it in his hand. It was huge for a cricket and terrifying. He wanted to take it home 'til he felt how mushy it had turned. When we reached an especially white patch of salt, I picked up a crystal the size of a rice grain and tasted the world. As bitter as it was clean. A couple hundred yards away, a series of white bumps extended into the lake.

15.

Yes, Spiral Jetty—and above the lake line, but only in places. Most of it buried in six to eighteen inches of water. Every inch of every exposed rock coated in thirty years of salt, and wherever we cast our shadows, shadowy blue. The jetty seemed worn out, art hardened back into landscape. Where was the early '70s jetty, the jetty I'd been carrying around in my head, the one I could run from beginning to end, with my own feet, just as I'd seen flesh-and-blood Smithson do? Or as flesh-and-blood as video allows: Smithson running the backbone of his creation. Or not running but hopping from rock to rock since the jetty even then was uneven, bigger boulders on the edges to anchor the smaller ones. Over the broken surface he goes, a helicopter capturing all this from above. Smithson, looking back over his shoulder, shoulder-length hair streaming. Is he being chased? Is this his celebration run after being marooned? Smithson hurrying now, turning inward, left, always to the left. Smithson stopping finally at the center, where there's nowhere else to go.

16.

Nothing prepares you for the color of the water. Like tomato soup, Smithson says, thanks to micro bacteria. Yes, but tomato soup made not with water or milk but cream. A salmon-y color you'd be happy to find in front of you in an Indian restaurant, thick with chunks of Tandoori chicken. An eerie, beautiful color licking salt-white boulders. I kept expecting to see a freshly slaughtered whale nearby. And glaciers. I kept expecting to feel cold.

17.

More than *see* Spiral Jetty, I wanted to *walk* it. To walk it, to run it, to hop from rock to rock as Smithson had, to circle inward and find myself at the end of something, winded and surrounded by water. Yes, we had brought extra shoes, as my friend had recommended, but I didn't think I'd need to wade the entire jetty. I put on ancient Nikes, Jacqui and Brooke pulled on snow boots and Derek surprised us all by staying on shore to look for Jerusalem crickets. At first we tried to keep dry, but there was danger in rock hopping, and soon the rocks would be too far apart, so we splashed into the cold water and began slogging through the salt. With each step, our feet sank a little. The jetty was a white underwater path, marked by the darker water on either side—red and murky and ominous. Ominous? How ridiculous, I thought. If I fall in, I fall in. Sure, I'd get wet, but the water was only four feet deep, if that. This was the pep talk I gave, first to myself, then to Brooke. The sensation kept creeping back: we're in the Arctic. The farther we walked out on the jetty, the more ice floes we saw. No, pieces of salt floating.

18.

Throughout the afternoon, lines from "Anecdote of the Jar" kept slipping into my mind. "It made the slovenly wilderness surround that hill" and "The wilderness rose up to it, and sprawled around, no longer wild." A Wallace Stevens poem I didn't much care for as a student, though it's grown on me since. A poem of liminal spaces and transformation. Which is how I think of Spiral Jetty: a jar Smithson and crew placed in a Tennessee called Utah, though somehow that gives too much agency to Smithson. Since arriving, I had come to think of Spiral Jetty less as Smithson's brainchild and more as lovely devastation—an odd, corkscrewing piece of civilization turned wild. And this tiny section of Great Salt Lake a natural place made richer and more problematic by human incursion.

19.

"Like wading in jewels," Jacqui said.
 Which was a romantic and beautiful way to say it, except that the smaller jewels kept getting in our shoes. Grittier than sand.

"They hurt my feet," Brooke said.

So we'd stop periodically, sit down on a rock and wash the salt crystals out of our shoes by sloshing them in water many times brinier than the ocean.

20.

I stopped at the outside rim of the spiral. Water wherever I looked. Smithson, staring at the same water, had conceived of Spiral Jetty. *An immobile cyclone. Flickering light. A landscape that appeared to quake. A dormant earthquake spread into the fluttering stillness. A spinning sensation without movement. A rotary that enclosed itself in an immense roundness.* Though I distrusted his tendency to skate for paragraphs from one abstract epiphany to another, largely leaving behind the landscape and a contextualizing eye, I did not distrust his underlying intuition. There was a fluttering stillness here. I scanned the horizon, cataloguing where it was I was. To the east, beyond the shore, the highway that had brought us here, and beyond that, the Wasatch Front. To the south: Antelope Island, too far away to see, where early settlers ran cattle and that was now home to a herd of buffalo, herded once a year into a corral where a man with a portable computer read the microchip in each left ear. To the west, the Salt Flats, where daredevils and engineers gathered yearly to squeeze a few more miles per hour out of rockets strapped to cars in hopes of breaking the land speed record. But those places were far away. I had to take them on faith. For now, I was on the edge of a landlocked ocean, the remnant of Lake Bonneville. Wispy clouds helped to delineate the sky. All I could hear was wind and the licking of water.

21.

Halfway toward the center of the jetty, we heard a hum from the west. Jacqui picked out a small plane. When it passed over, dipping its wing for a better view, we waved.

After its fourth pass, Brooke asked, "Is he trying to get us in trouble?"

"No," Jacqui said, "just looking."

Looking, but from far away. And here we were, wading. Wading and complaining about salt crystals in our shoes and feeling found and then lost again. How many works from art history let you walk all over them? It struck me then that the people in the plane were completing a lazy museum stroll, albeit from a private plane. And our waving was part of their *Spiral Jetty*.

22.

Tired, bored, her feet hurting, Brooke sat down on a giant mushroom of salt to wait. There were fewer boulders now to mark the edges. Jacqui and I walked along without her, keeping to the salt path. All at once, dark water on three sides instead of two. We stopped. Part of me wanted to step into the deep. Jacqui kissed me.
"What was that for?"
"Bragging rights," she said.

23.

I am tempted now, as I wasn't then, to draw conclusions. To say that Spiral Jetty is like Crick and Watson's double helix. Like Yeats's falcon, turning and turning in a widening gyre. Like Hitchcock's *Vertigo*. Like the whiteout my father experienced on a highway in an Idaho snowstorm, so disoriented he pulled over and closed his eyes to prove he wasn't moving. Like a journey that takes you where you want to go by going somewhere else. Smithson himself said it was like the portrait Brancusi drew of James Joyce as nautilus shell. It took twenty-five minutes to wade to the end of the jetty (or was it the beginning?), fifteen to wade back to shore. Spiral Jetty is like all these things and none of them. As Emily Dickinson said, "We both believe, and disbelieve a hundred times an Hour, which keeps Believing nimble."

24.

"Look," Derek said as we neared shore. He pointed to a giant smiley face he'd drawn in salt and, beside it, his own spiral jetty. Then at a rock. "Before, it had feathers sticking out from under it, so I started digging. Underneath I found another dead pelican. I buried it again but deeper. Now no one can tell." "Any other creatures?" I asked. "Nope," he said. "Too salty."

25.

We rinsed off our legs the best we could with drinking water and changed our shoes. Or, rather, Jacqui and Brooke changed theirs. I kept my squishy

Nikes on. We drank some juice and then began the hike up the hill to see the jetty from above. I held myself back from looking, willing myself forward another fifty yards, a hundred yards. I liked the restraint, seeing by looking away. We followed a horse trail, dodging manure, and kept climbing through the bitter hot smell of sagebrush. We stopped and turned around. We were seeing the same picture we had just been a part of, the same picture we had shown the kids a week before, at breakfast, when we explained the trip. Our younger son, five, whom we had left home, had seen the picture from across the table. He thought it was a giant question mark in the sky. When he learned a jetty sits in water, he cried.

Most things, I wanted to tell him, just "sit in water" until inflected by context. By wet feet and hunger, by legs itchy with dried salt and by a giant question mark touching down from the sky like a tornado and by Derek yelling, "I almost got him," then running toward us with his thumb and finger lifted, as if in blessing. In his hand he held a piece of lizard tail the color of earth, twitching still, as if it had a mind of its own.

Chapter 3

THE GARDEN

by James R. West

March 20 marks the first day of spring, and no matter what the weather's like, workers across the Washington, D.C. metro area are out spreading a special mixture of fertilizer. They put it on the flower beds, over dead spots of grass and around trees and bushes. I wake up to the smell every year and wander around my apartment looking for rotten milk until I recognize the source, but the smell takes me all the way back to the spring of 1974 in Ogden, Utah.

That year, my parents rented a two-bedroom house from the Smiths a half block south of Fortieth Street on Monroe Avenue. It was in a modest Utah neighborhood and the first house I remember. Moving from the shared space with my dad's mother in Rawlins, Wyoming, my mom was eager to have a place of her own. She didn't seem to mind that instead of a lawn, this place came with a half acre of dirt.

The dirt lot was an eyesore in a neighborhood where dark green lawns mowed to golf-course perfection signified something more than just skillful maintenance. It was a matter of pride and status. Evidence of a previous lawn at this house had dried up and blown away long ago since the landlord, Mr. Smith, seemed to have other priorities than to spend money or his Saturdays on lawn care.

My dad saw potential in the dirt lot. We were in the house less than a week when my dad made the announcement at dinner.

"I'm going to plant a garden," he said. "And Jimmy is going to help me."

"That sounds nice," my mother said. "Maybe you can plant one when we get our own place."

Utah Reflections

Ben Lomond Peak behind the clouds. *Photo credit Jason Chacon.*

Mount Ogden in the winter. It sits like a memento of the quickly changing seasons. *Photo credit Jason Chacon.*

Friday evening, Dad came home from work with tall wooden stakes and kite string. We plotted out the area in front of the house for the garden before sunset. From the porch steps, my mother watched, her arms folded.

"You can't just plop down a garden in the middle of the neighborhood. Mr. Smith will never have it."

"We'll see," Dad said.

The next morning, I was at the table eating Cheerios when my other grandma—my mom's mother—came by in her shiny black Cadillac to pick up my mom and younger brother, Tommy. They were going to Salt Lake City to visit my aunt and great-grandma. As they drove away, Dad put down his paper and told me to put on my boots.

We watered down the plotted-out garden area, and soon after, Farmer Jenkins pulled into the driveway. The truck, noticeably overloaded, rocked side to side as it came up the driveway. Farmer Jenkins lined up the truck and extended the bed over the kite string boundary. When the tailgate dropped, manure poured onto the ground. The smell was unbearable. Dad and Farmer Jenkins started to move the manure with a pitchfork and shovel. I stood near the tailgate and held my nose.

"Ugh! What's that smell?"

"It's manure," Farmer Jenkins said. He grabbed a handful and smashed it around in his glove. It was a clot of green dirt mixed with hay and grass.

"Manure?"

"Horse shit," Dad said, laughing.

Farmer Jenkins held it up to his nose. "Good stuff!"

I stared at my dad in disbelief. The smell didn't seem to bother him as he shoveled more manure out onto the ground.

"Secret ingredient, son. This is what makes gardens grow," he said.

"Yuck." I decided to watch them from the porch.

By lunchtime, the manure had been spread, and Farmer Jenkins had unloaded a rototiller machine for my dad to use. I tried not to breathe as we ate peanut butter sandwiches and watched as a rotating sprinkler wet the new garden area. Flies had shown up long before lunchtime, and now they buzzed wildly around our heads.

"The next step is mixing the manure into the soil with the rototiller. Gardens only grow if you prepare them right," Dad said. He instructed me to go grab the bag in the milk crate by the garage door. Inside the bag were several different boxes and packets of seeds. Dad picked up a small box and shook it like a rattle.

"Corn," he said. He picked up another box. "Peas." Then a packet. "Cucumbers. Squash. And the very best—tomatoes."

"I like corn," I said.

"For me, I would say my favorite has to be tomatoes." He paused, sighed and looked at me to really get my attention. "You can't grow them at Grandma's house in Wyoming, you know."

"No manure?" I said.

"The summer isn't long enough for the tomatoes to get ripe."

A world without tomatoes sounded pretty good to me.

After lunch, we continued to water. The afternoon sun beat down, and the steam intensified the smell. I couldn't water, pull the hose and hold my nose at the same time—I had to breathe through my mouth. When we were done, we pulled the hoses back to the house and rolled them up.

"Jimmy," Dad said, "hold my glasses."

He untucked his T-shirt from his belted jeans and then pulled it off over his head. He splashed his face with water and wiped it with his shirt. I looked around nervously to see if anyone could see him and waited for my dad to put his shirt back on. Instead, he walked to the porch, bare-chested, and draped his shirt over the porch rail. I handed him back his glasses, and he put them on along with his gloves. He clapped his gloves together.

"Well, let's get this rototiller fired up and mix this garden!" he said.

I was mortified.

Bending down to prime the gas tank, Dad waved me over. "Come on. I want to show you how to run this thing." He must have seen the look on my face.

"What's wrong?" he asked.

"You're naked! You're naked outside!"

"Naked?" he replied. "I'm not naked. I'm ready to work."

He stood up and pulled his gloves tighter over his hands. He made a fist and held it up like a boxer.

"Today, we work with our shirts off!" He flexed his arms, the muscles standing out. Then he gave his best bandito impression. "*We don't need no stinking shirts!*"

I couldn't get my shirt off fast enough. I flexed my arms and growled and repeated the bandito shirt rule until we both laughed.

Dad pulled the starter cord on the rototiller, and it started up with a roar. The heavy machine jumped and bounced as it churned through the dirt. Hanging on to the handles, Dad looked like he had a bull by the horns trying to keep it from gouging him. He wrestled the tiller back and forth over the garden, making long rows through the wet soil and mixing in the manure. I followed him with my shirt off, walking in the wet manure and dirt that spewed out behind him. It felt great to be a man.

My job was to pick out the rocks as they were tilled up to the surface. When the bucket was full, I would empty it at the edge of the yard next to the fence. During one of my full-bucket runs, my new friend Steve and his little sister were standing at the fence. They were both pinching their noses shut.

"Why do you have your shirt off?"

"We're working."

"On what?"

"Planting a garden."

"In your front yard?"

I turned around and looked at the garden and then over at the manicured lawn in front of Steve's house and across the street at the Millers' tight, green lawn. I shrugged my shoulders and dumped my bucket of rocks.

Steve's sister, nose held shut, gave a nasal whine. "Are you guys poor?"

"No, stupid," I said. "We can afford a garden."

They both looked down at my boots covered with manure and dirt.

"*You're* stupid," Steve's sister said.

I never liked Steve's sister.

James West stands with his brother near their childhood garden. *Photo credit Roy West.*

"Can you play?" Steve asked.

"No. I'm working. See you tomorrow in church."

The rototiller went silent when it ran out of fuel. Dad let me hold the gas can, and while we were refueling, a car drove past on Monroe Avenue and honked twice. The Hamilton girls from church both shouted out the window, "Woooo!"

"Why were they yelling?" I asked.

"They must be smelling the manure," Dad said.

Throughout the rest of the afternoon, more cars went by, honking or with shout-outs, "Whoo hoo!" or "Yeeeeeaahh!" My dad waved without looking the first couple of times, but after that, he ignored the hoots. He focused on the even rows of the garden. I waved at every one of the cars. People sure were excited about our garden.

Sister Craner came over. She was our new neighbor and also my primary teacher at church, which is why we called her "Sister." She held a Fresca in one hand and, with the other, covered her mouth and nose with a daisy-printed hanky. My dad turned off the rototiller and greeted her, waving a muddy glove.

"Hello, Sister Craner."

"I had to walk down and see if a garbage truck had overturned," she said. "I was trying to do some yard work myself, but it actually smells worse downwind."

"Sorry about that," my dad said, not sounding very sorry. "I needed to fertilize this dead soil."

"A garden, huh? How *pioneer* of you," she said. I thought she might have actually rolled her eyes. "Most wives just want a lawn and a flower bed."

My dad pulled the cord on the rototiller. The sound drowned out anything else Sister Craner had to say, and she went away without saying goodbye.

When the rototilling was done, we raked, staked and hoed the dirt into long perfect rows that resembled racetrack lanes at a Pinewood derby event. For the planting, I followed my dad as he sowed the seeds. With one quick motion, he made a hole with his planting stick and dropped in a seed. I smoothed dirt over the top and gave each seed two pats. Three rows of corn, two rows of peas, one row of carrots, cucumbers and squash. The tomatoes we planted in one corner of the garden so they would have more room to grow. Dad skewered the packets onto stakes at the top of each row to designate what was planted.

When the planting was finished, we stood at the edge of the garden and watched the water from the hoses fill the little moats between each row and slowly sink into the soil. I couldn't wait to see the garden grow. I remember wondering how tall the corn would be by the next morning.

It was late afternoon when my grandma's black Cadillac pulled into the driveway. She and my mom and brother Tommy all stared out the windows at the new landscape. As the electric car window came down with that electric-motor sound, the look on Grandma's face changed from curiosity to something sour. She got out of the car, fanning at the air.

"We made a garden!" I shouted.

Tommy jumped out from the backseat and pointed at my chest. "I can see your *chi-chis*!"

Grandma began to giggle. She glanced at me and then my dad. "I can see everyone's *chi-chis*."

"Where's your shirt?" Mom snapped. She was pointing at me, but she was glaring at my dad.

Nothing else needed to be said. Dad and I walked to the porch and grabbed our shirts.

"We're going to share our vegetables with you," I told Grandma.

"That's wonderful," she said, her giggle turning into her signature snort-giggle. "I guess your dad hasn't been to the grocery store lately." She blew me a kiss as she got back into her car and drove away.

My mom was watching Dad as he pretended to be busy perfecting one of the rows with a hoe.

"How do you like our garden?" I asked her.

"It's…" she said. She tried to smile. "It's a big garden. I mean, really big!"

Tommy was at the far end of the garden on his knees, scooping mud with a stick. He had taken his shirt off, and it was partially in the mud and partially under his knees. His chubby belly squeezed out over his belt.

Mom looked at him and bit her lip. She pointed at my dad. "You better hose these boys off before they take one step into my house. Leave the boots, socks, pants and shirts in the washroom." She stalked into the house.

Dad checked to make sure she was gone, and then he smiled at me.

"I guess we *do* need our stinking shirts." We both laughed.

Tommy and I floated leaves down the moats between the rows of planted seeds and played in the dirt around the garden until the sun began to set. Mr. Smith came over, along with Mr. Miller from across the street, and I stood near the men, pretending to understand their conversation. They pointed, laughed and talked about fertilizer, different types of corn and the perfect tomato. Mr. Smith didn't seem to mind the garden at all. When it was almost too dark to see, they shook Dad's hand and went home. Tommy and I followed Dad into the house.

Our family had several gardens over the years, huge gardens in each of the two suburban houses my parents bought. Manure was spread. Shirts were worn. But after that first one, none of the gardens was ever in the front yard, only in the back.

Eventually, the excitement of a garden turned into a chore. Garden chores cut into my time with friends and Saturday morning cartoons. Dad had to push us to "keep up" with the garden. And every year, without fail, when the fall harvest made its way to our table, he would announce in his best Little Red Hen voice, "Who will help me *eat* the corn?"

That night after we'd planted the first garden, after a bath, after dinner and prayers, I lay in my bed exhausted. Tommy was already asleep, but as tired as I was, I felt wide awake. A cool breeze flowed through the house, fluttering the curtains. Dad stuck his head into my room, and across the hall in my parents' room, a window slid shut with a bang. Dad just smiled.

"Good job today," he said. He turned off the bedroom light and closed the door almost all the way until only a thin line of light shined through the crack. We'd made a garden, my dad and I, and it was better than anything else we could've done that day. I guess I'd even gotten used to the smell because it didn't bother me anymore.

Chapter 4

THE PIT BULL AND THE MOUNTAIN GOAT

by Pam Houston

I remember the first time I drove into Park City. It was ten years ago next September, the day was cool and sunny, the sky from horizon to horizon a shade I've since come to think of as Utah blue. I noticed Osgood Thorpe's Dairy Barn first, the whitewashed sideboards and weather vanes, and the ocean of fields he owned around it. Behind the barn was a mountain of aspen trees, nearly all gone yellow, and the scrub oak, glowing red, and the evergreens. Snaking down the mountain and through the trees were the ski runs: Prospector, King Consolidated, Glory Hole, Pay Day, runs I would ski so many times in the next ten years I'd forget that their names referred to anything besides steeps and bumps and fresh Utah powder. I'd forget that in those names lay the reason Park City was built in the first place: silver mines and the men who worked them. It took me about five minutes to fall in love with their ramshackle Victorian houses and the rickety stairways they built to climb the canyon walls between them, the abandoned mine shafts and the stained-glass windows, the old whorehouse and the train station and all the other ghosts the miners had left behind.

I'd been living in Salt Lake City, under the inversion layer and the eyes of my Mormon neighbors, having signed on to a five-year PhD program at the University of Utah. My teachers and colleagues said if I moved to Park City all I'd do is ski and drink and sit in the sun and walk in the mountains. They said I'd stop coming to classes, stop writing papers, I probably wouldn't even get my degree. All I knew was that the air was clean and you could see all the stars at night, and every house I looked at had a path out the back where you could put on your skis and ski right down to the town lift.

Utah Reflections

I rented a one-hundred-year-old house straight out of Munchkinland with no insulation, doorways I had to duck to get through and floors that sloped a different direction in every room down and away from some high point in the center. When the snow and ice slid off the tin roof, it made a noise that had me swearing the house was splitting down the middle, as it will one day soon I'm sure. I learned to cook with the woodstove that the house had been built around in 1898, and I dug bottles out of my garden that were handmade from thick colored glass and stamped, like money. My neighbor across the street was the genuine article, an ancient miner who hooked himself up to an oxygen tank for four hours every day to fight the silicosis in his lungs. He fell in love with my dog Hailey and fed her white bread and fried chicken even after I told him the vet forbade it. I took long walks with the dogs all over the mountain, learning the names of the ski runs, standing on the fall lines, willing it to snow.

My life became enormously uncomplicated in Park City. I would get up when the sun hit my bedroom window, which was around six o'clock in the summer and eight in the winter and not at all on those very few days a year when the sun didn't shine. I would write until I got bored with myself and then walk down to the Morning Ray for coffee and muffins and then on down Main Street to the post office. I would stop by and pet the cat at Dolly's bookstore and visit Peter Snosnowski, who cuts my hair, and then I'd walk up the hill and go to work.

When the snow started to fall and the lifts opened, I was out there every morning, carving fresh turns down Assessment, Powder Keg and Blue Slip Bowl. I didn't take Utah snow for granted in those days, and each morning, the feathery arcs my skis kicked up seemed like brand-new miracles, the soundless, weightless sensation of moving through snow that came all the way across a desert to fall in my backyard. If it wasn't a powder day, there'd be a better-than-ever chance I'd make it to my literature class. Sometimes I didn't move my truck for several days at a time.

I remember that first year on the mountain, the uncrowded December days, when I'd pick one chairlift a day and ski all the runs 'til I had them memorized: the trees on the left of Thaynes Run kept the bumps soft there until late in the day, but the Hoist was where the real bump skiers carved the best lines. I remember my first day up into Jupiter Bowl, Park City's lift-accessed expert-only terrain, my first tentative turns down the West Face on an early powder day watching for stumps and rocks and then the first moment of letting go, of giving my weight to the mountain. I remember the first time I hiked to the top of Scott's Bowl, the highest accessible point on

Park City Mountains. *Photo credit Kathryn Hale.*

the mountain, the first time I let my skis drop off its big cornice, the feeling of landing in something not quite bottomless but a very long way from solid ground. I remember my first time in the steeper MacConkey's Bowl, scared and back so far on my skis I snapped the buckle off my boot, missed a turn and tumbled five hundred vertical feet before I came to rest, skiless and poleless with one boot halfway off, but whole and grinning like a cartoon snow creature at my friends' enthusiastic round of applause.

I came to love Scott's Bowl the best; though I never got very good at skiing it, I loved to stand at the top of it and look out at the whole Wasatch Front stretched before me in one direction and the wetland meadows where the sandhill cranes made their homes in the other, at Mount Timpanogos, the sleeping princess, behind me, and everywhere acres of untracked snow. I loved the drop off the cornice, the turns down the face that was the perfect amount of steep, for powder, for crud, for me. I loved knowing I had the long trip to the base ahead of me, loved knowing how easy the groomers would feel after skiing the bowl, how soft and immaculate Silver Queen would be, how fast I could take the last turn (the only turn) down Nastar.

I learned that first year, too, the legends of Park City, not just the legends of the old days and the silver boom but the new ones the young town was creating. There was Dan McCann, for instance, the best skier and mountaineer in town, who amazed everyone by being the first man to climb and ski 12,800 feet of Mount Timpanogos, all in one short winter day. The best bar in town then was Cisero's basement on Wednesday, jam night, though any of the rugby players would tell you it was the Alamo, and they ought to know, being legendary themselves. The best meal in town was at Adolph's, if you could afford it, and if you couldn't, the best deal was back at Cisero's, local spaghetti night, all you could eat for $5.95. Most people agreed that the best-looking men in town were the Peek brothers, who did carpentry out of the backs of their pickup trucks and occasionally put the money together to buy, refurbish and sell a house. The best cup of coffee was and always will be at the Morning Ray. The best day of the year back then was Clown Day, April 1, when all the locals dressed as clowns and ate mushrooms and skied their brains out in the perfect spring corn snow, pushing the bumps aside as they went, giggling their heads off. The best nights were in the off-season when there was no work and even less money, and we'd gather on porches to tell stories and sing and play guitar.

The off-season was a good time to get up high in the mountains, too, and after almost ten years of driving through the Heber Valley and looking up at Mount Timpanogos—of studying the figure of the sleeping princess, of waiting for the first autumn morning when she is dusted in snow, of watching the snowfield on the northeasternmost slope melt into the horse's head that signals the planting of corn in the valley—after years of more or less worshipping that mountain, I finally took the time to climb it. I was with my oldest friend, Kelly, who lives in Chicago, and who was thinking of making the big move out west.

I took her up Timpanogos because I wanted to show her how easy it is for us to get into the wilderness, how it's right there in our backyards whenever we need it, how sometimes we don't realize we need it until we are there. But halfway up the trail, I thought I had made a mistake. First there was the graffiti, scrawled across every sign and available rock, and when we started to climb, every switchback had been crosscut two or three times; on the flat part, eight or sometimes ten trails reached across the meadows.

In a western state where a relatively small percentage of the population actually goes hiking, the damage I saw was staggering. I was ashamed of the way that trail had been treated, ashamed that I had taken Kelly to a place not pristine at all but scarred and ugly. I was working up an apology, some way of convincing her that not all the trails in Utah are like this, when she said, "This is absolutely the most incredibly beautiful place I have ever seen in my life."

And when I lifted my head and looked more than ten feet beyond my hiking boots, I knew, of course, that she was right. There we were, in a massive glacial cirque, surrounded on three sides by vertical granite walls and on the fourth by more wildflowers than the average Chicagoan could ever dream of: Indian paintbrush, every shade from the palest yellow through the oranges and into the deepest red; purple fireweed; white, pink and multicolored columbine; lavender bluebells. Beyond the flowers stood the rest of the Wasatch Mountains and, beyond those, the high Uintas. I was busy looking at outhouse trails and boot marks while all around me was the definition of sublime.

After another couple of hours of climbing, Kelly and I arrived at the top of Timpanogos—at the funny little metal house that must have been important to someone—and sat down for a drink. We got our first real look down the populated side of the mountain, and there was Orem spread below us, with its belching smokestacks, and Provo, at rush hour in fact, traffic all backed up along Interstate 15. We heard car horns blowing clear as a bell even there where we sat, almost eight thousand feet above them. We watched a golden eagle make lazy circles between us and the city, and I stirred up some coyote scat that lay on the trail in front of me and wondered what could possibly live up this high on the windy, barren face of the mountain that a coyote would come all this way to eat. That's when I saw the sunlight catch the flash of two pointy black horns, and the bushy white back end of an animal moved behind a rock not three hundred feet in front of me.

"Did you see that?" I said to Kelly. But she shook her head.

"I know this sounds crazy," I said, "but I swear I just saw a mountain goat, not ten feet from the trail where we just climbed."

We watched and waited until the patriarch wandered back into our view. He was a big ram, and an old ram, and we watched him settle his big body down in a small rock niche overlooking the smokestacks and traffic patterns, overlooking the smog.

"I can't believe it," I said to Kelly. "Of all the places, why would those goats want to live here?"

Mountain goats are shy creatures that, given the option, like to live in places where people don't ever go, and I was thinking about all the hikers, the dogs and children, who traverse the trail daily. I was thinking about the horse-pack trips, the train whistles and fire sirens, the fact that of all the trails in Utah, Timpanogos was probably the most heavily used.

"He probably likes the lights," Kelly said quietly. "At night, the city lights must be awesome from up here."

We looked around the green meadow immediately below and realized we were surrounded by mountain goats, at least twenty ewes and lambs. While we were watching the ram, they had all come out to graze, and we watched for a long time, their white coats catching the setting sunlight, the city lights down below.

Kelly and I got off the mountain way too late that night—so late, in fact, that we had to hold hands and feel our way down the switchbacks in the dark, so late that my roommate had Search and Rescue halfway up the mountain before we could get to a phone and say we had made it just fine. Kelly was long gone back to Chicago before I understood why we had sat there so long watching the mountain goats when we knew we had six miles to hike back to the car.

It had to do with Park City and the complaining we'd all been doing about the changes that had come on our town too fast and furious to comprehend. We sat in our cars out on Highway 224 all summer breathing one another's exhaust, eye to eye with a manhole cover, trying to imagine driving the new road, wide and high above the valley, no longer getting a feel for the lay of the land. We watched the construction of one big concrete structure after another as if they were mirages, remembering the sandhill cranes that used to migrate through those meadows, wondering what store we needed that we had lived so long without.

A new Wal-Mart opens up in America every two days. We were bound to get one eventually. Still, we felt somehow different from the rest of America, and in our difference, we thought we were immune. We weren't. And it was difficult to count the ways all the development affected us. We didn't recognize anybody at the Albertsons anymore. And who were those people in their new Ford Explorers who didn't even smile and wave? We had our mountain bikes/tape decks/Ray-Bans stolen, and that would have never happened two or six or ten years ago. We were moaning about rental prices, but we'd all worked for less than ten dollars an hour forever, and who had the money to buy? Our years of hoping we wouldn't become another Aspen were behind us; for better or worse, Park City had arrived.

This was what we deserved, our yuppie siblings and disapproving parents told us, for living the way we did; and now, having seen Park City through its fledgling years, there was nothing to do except move on to some other town, where rent was cheap and work was plentiful and we could start all over again. Unless, of course, we were too stubborn to leave. Unless we looked at the fact that we had spent most of our adult lives making a home here and we were invested in saying the things about Park City that would allow us to stay.

We came here, many of us, in our twenties, when everything we owned fit into the back of a Honda Civic, and now we'd need Allied Van Lines to cart it away. We were attached to Park City in ways we'd never fully comprehend until we moved. In so many important respects, we grew up here, and when I saw that goat hovering on the thin ridge of mountain between Sundance and Provo, I decided I wouldn't give up on Park City without a fight. I decided that if I could always see the wildflowers, I could learn to love the city lights, and that was enough to keep me here, for a while.

I found out a few days after our hike that the mountain goats were introduced successfully onto Mount Timpanogos in 1981, the year before I first came to Utah, and that they have been thriving there ever since. A few days after that, I heard another story about the goats that bears repeating.

A friend of mine named Ben went up Timpanogos with a backpack to spend the night near the windy summit. When he got there, he met another man, also making a camp for the night, who had brought a pit bull with him up the trail. The two men set up camp about a half mile away from each other, and at dusk, when the goats came out to graze, Ben watched the other man sic his pit bull on the old patriarch, saying, "Kill! Kill!"—the command for the pit bull to lock his jaws.

Ben knew the man was carrying a bottle of Jack Daniel's and not one but two pistols, but he moved forward anyway to try to intervene. He'd only got within swinging distance of the man with the guns when he saw what the goat was doing. Like some kind of Asian fan dancer, the goat would lower his horns and pull the dog closer and closer to the edge of the cliff, waiting a little longer to jump sideways or upward to the next rock ledge each time the dog lunged. The dog got more and more excited, less and less sensible, until finally the goat waited just long enough to send the dog hurtling seven hundred feet over the cliff.

Ben watched while the man climbed down and retrieved his dog, while he carried the dog's bloody body back to his camp. The dog was still alive then, and Ben asked if there was anything he could do to help, but the dog owner said the dog would be fine, and Ben went back to his tent alone. By the next morning, the whiskey bottle was empty, the man was gone and the dog was dead.

I spent a year after the Timpanogos hike living and teaching in Ohio in a place where the Wal-Mart-to-wilderness ratio is about a thousand to one. I walked—and I really believe this—every hiking trail in Ohio. None of them took more than half a day; all of them wound up in somebody's backyard. And what did I trade for the wilderness? I was forty-five minutes from a decent bookstore, an hour from an interesting restaurant, three hours from a professional sports team of any kind and sixteen hundred miles from any snow worth skiing. I couldn't get a good cup of coffee, I couldn't buy Pepperidge Farm cookies at the grocery store, there was no such thing as Mexican food and the most complicated movie I could see without driving a long way was *Honey I Shrunk the Kids*.

I missed Park City so badly that year that I even missed the things I don't like. I got sentimental about standing in line at the post office; my heart would race when I heard Orrin Hatch's name on TV. And all those things I thought I'd be so happy to get away from—the Christmas-week lift lines and the 5:00 a.m. trips to the Albertsons—seemed like awfully small reasons to move away.

I'm not saying I could accept the changes that were coming to Park City, any more than I could accept the way people had trashed the Timpanogos trail, and I'm sure even then I could see the time coming when I'd give up on Park City for good. But the trip to Ohio reminded me to look beyond my own hiking boots, to not lose sight of the things that were still good in Park City, things I knew we would have to keep track of, or we were bound to lose them too.

Like the way it feels that first day in November when the kind of snowflakes start to fall that make me say, "Tune the skis; we're hiking up to Jupiter tomorrow." Like the particular blue of an early April sky when I'm coming down Prospector face all alone, pushing the soft bumps out of my way as I go. Like the fireworks exploding through the Thanksgiving snowflakes while the band America sings my high school prom theme for the millionth time. Like Christmas week, when we are all almost too burned out to be civil to one another, but we manage to come together, sometime between when the bars close and the lifts open, to decorate the tree and toast the new year. Like the summer symphony at Deer Valley, drinking wine and watching night fall on the forest while one hundred violinists play "Carolina in the Pines." Those are the times when I thought, "This is my town, and it's the best place I will ever be."

And if there was a lesson to be learned from the story of the pit bull, surely it lay in the tenacity of the goat. A goat that continued to hang in there, in spite of pollution, of traffic, of car horns and one sick man with a pit bull. Like almost all of us, that goat was a transplant, and he must have known it could be worse; if he couldn't work it out on Timpanogos, he might have wound up in Ohio. He was a goat that learned to roll with the changes, and more important, maybe, he learned that—locking jaws notwithstanding— he was a smart enough goat to drive a pit bull over a cliff.

But Park City has changed a lot even since the day I saw the goats on Timpanogos, and I'm not as tenacious as they are, even though I might like to be. Tasteful, modern Victorian-looking condos have replaced too many of the old crumbling houses. We got a K-Mart to go with our Wal-Mart, and a mall full of outlet stores has made it impossible for even the most enterprising sandhill crane to land. I don't find any more old glass bottles or five-cent Campbell's soup cans when I go walking with the dogs. The back of every ski pass in Park City now reads, "Full and midweek season passes are not valid on April 1 or any other day when a season pass holder is dressed or made up as a clown," and most people who hold season passes these days have no idea why. The miner across the street died five years ago, but his angry wife still comes through for Hailey. "Come here, you son of a bitch," she screams out her front door, and Hailey waggles over and takes an entire loaf of three-day-old Wonder bread in her mouth. Osgood Thorpe's barn still stands, though the million-dollar houses are encroaching. Rumor has it that it took years and a big pile of money before he sold the county enough property to widen the last stretch of the road.

I know people who wind up leaving a place they've lived in a long time because they say they've outgrown it. But I'm leaving Park City because

Park City Barn sits beneath the shallow slope of a mountainside. *Photo credit Kathryn Hale.*

Skiing swirls down the Peak Canyons. *Photo credit Aric Russom.*

it's outgrown me. In the ten years I've been in Park City, its population has increased 500 percent. The Morning Ray is three times its original size, the Peek brothers are millionaires, Peter has his own salon now and calls himself Peter Anthony, Dolly's burned down and has been rebuilt and they have a brand-new cat that sits in the window. We have espresso now, and sushi, and bars with bands that are actually worth paying money to see. We have fine art in the galleries and clothes from four continents and twenty-four-hour taxis and Federal Express. Park City is a world-class resort now; it's me who's still a little rough around the edges, and I'm bound to find someplace new that's at least as scruffy as I am.

I leave Park City grateful for my years there, for the comfort I found in a place whose every nook and cranny became as familiar to me as drawing a breath. My teachers were right, of course. I never did finish my PhD. But I did learn something anyway about what's important in my life: a stand of aspen trees, still green but just about to go golden, and first turns on a bright blue morning after the high desert angels have been making powder all night.

Chapter 5
THE CURLING FINGERS OF THE HATCH WOMEN

by Jana Richman

Shortly after my forty-eighth birthday, I moved home to Utah. I had been gone more than twenty years—some of it in New York City, most of it in Tucson. I returned to pursue love with the man who is now my husband, and I returned to be with my mother at the end of her life—both solidly good reasons for moving back to Utah. But mostly, I returned because I spent my childhood in the shadow of the Oquirrhs, because I became an adult in the shadow of the Wasatch and because those mountains hold the knowledge of the person I was, the person I could have been and the person I am. I always knew I would return.

One spring day, a few years before my mother died, I sat at the kitchen table in my childhood home in Tooele, Utah, and skimmed a newspaper while my mother prepared a lesson she was to give in church on Sunday. As her left hand brushed over the pages of a Book of Mormon, only the tips of her fingers and the base of her wrist made contact with the delicate paper; she was unable to rest her hand flat upon the page. Her right hand curled around a pen, and she slowly and painfully made notes, rings glittering incongruously on the bent claw. Now, almost six years after her death, I still remember the feel of her curled hand in mine—loose skin, protruding veins, twisted knuckles. Under the pretense of comforting her, I used to stroke her hand, seeking solace for myself.

I noticed the curled hands of the Hatch women—my mother and her three sisters—as if they were spring-loaded and tripped overnight, first Agatha, followed in age order by Carrell, Leona and my mother, Darlene.

The wild grasses of the valleys sit below the mountains of the Wasatch Front. *Photo credit Jason Chacon.*

All four women had the curling fingers of my grandmother, Ethel Hatch. The Hatch women blamed the Gooch women—my grandmother's sisters and her mother—but it is a Hatch trait now, and I will unfortunately but proudly carry it forward. Shortly before I turned forty, when I started to feel pain at the base of my thumbs, I began to ask about the hands. My mother and aunts shrugged, as if I were asking why the sun rises or why the seasons change.

Every morning now, my hands scrabble with containers of calcium tablets, fish oil softgels, glucosmine chondroitin capsules and a host of antioxidant vitamins before I lackadaisically pop them in my mouth. I put no faith in the pills, the low-fat diet, the walking regime, the yoga, the bio-identical hormone-replacement therapy, green tea or a multitude of herbs I've tried in the past seventeen years while the pain in my hands has intensified. They are Hatch hands, now curled, as if they hold a fond memory of gripping a Ball fruit jar filled with pear halves.

I never saw my grandmother's hands before they began to curl. They fascinated me, all the things they could do in that condition. I saw them black with dirt from digging potatoes, I saw them red and raw from scrubbing pots and, later, I saw them resigned and lifeless, hanging over the arms of a wheelchair, jeweled with a single gold band, but I never saw them straight and strong.

At the Sunshine Terrace rest home in Logan, Utah, where my grandmother spent her final days, she would ask to be wheeled to the patio to sit among birds and honeysuckle, the sickly sweet smell of which would call forth memories. Mom and I sat on either side of her, a hand placed lightly on one of her knotted claws as they rested on the chair's cold steel. One side of my grandmother's face was paralyzed, blinded and deafened by the accident that took her husband when she was forty-four, and whenever she got ready to tell a story, she would twist her head and fix her good eye on me, offer up her sad half-smile and speak in the cheerless voice of an old woman who had finished life long before her body would acknowledge it. A certain part of those stories remains uncomfortably lodged in me—as was her intent—like a piece of rotting wood in the sludge of a drying riverbed: the unbroken chain of never-idle hands in service to God and the Mormon Church.

★ ★ ★

My great-great-grandmother Anna Maria Larsen was twenty-nine years old and pregnant when she placed her young hands on the splintering holds of a handcart piled high with food, cooking utensils and bedding. Encountering rain, wind, dust and insects, she and her husband, Hans, averaged 15 miles a day, pulling the cart 1,300 miles along the Mormon Trail from Iowa City to Salt Lake City. Anna Maria settled in Brigham City and gave birth to eight children, five of whom died as infants. "Needed by God" is the notation next to their names in the family history. She began a lifelong work of sewing men's suits and women's dresses, her young daughter, Mary Ann, by her side, threading needles for her mother with nimble fingers.

Years later, Mary Ann Gooch, my great-grandmother, put her mother's teaching to use sewing burial clothes. In her capacity as a Relief Society member of the Mormon Church in Rich, Idaho, she embraced her duties to care for the dead.

> *With the body stretched out on the dining room table, Mary Ann ordered a bowl of warm, soapy water and one of cold water, sent the family out of the room and stripped the corpse naked. She placed a cold, wet cloth over the face then stepped down to take a look at the toes. She returned to the head, placed a small bundle on the table next to the right ear, tugged at the string*

and unrolled the pouch. She chose a pair of sewing scissors kept sharp by her husband, Belton Gooch, to clip the hard, yellow overgrown toenails. Mary Ann dropped her hands into the basin of warm, soapy water, hesitated for a moment and then pulled them out to wring a wet rag between her fingers. She scrubbed between the toes then moved up the body, unfolding skin and swabbing crevices. She paused midway to replace the face cloth with a fresh one so the face would not darken to the color of a blueberry stain. With the tip of the scissors, she dug dirt from under the nails, polished them with a wire brush and cut them close to the finger. Mary Ann then dressed the body, bundled up her tools and stepped quietly past the family as she massaged the palm of one aching hand with the fingers of the other.

In the only photograph I have of her, Mary Ann Gooch seems to look straight at me. She is a more stalwart-looking woman than her daughter, my grandmother. As I look at the photo, I place a finger over the softball-sized goiter protruding below her right ear, above her collar. The face is solemn but not unpleasant. When I remove my finger, the face becomes stern, almost frightening. There are worse things to inherit than aching hands.

My grandmother's own life followed the pattern sewn by her mother and grandmother—a life of service to others. She raised eight children, her youngest—my mother—only thirteen when she lost her husband. She cooked meals and washed dishes at the Sigma Chi fraternity house at Utah State University, and she took care of old women in their homes until she needed the same herself.

Grandmother ended each story she told with a firm caution: the devil and idle hands work together. Then she often recited this nursery rhyme:

I have two little hands so soft and white
This is the left and this is the right.
Five little fingers standing on each
So they can hold a plum or a peach.
When I get as big as you
Lots of things these little hands can do.

"I've never been idle" were her words to me, and when she said them, I knew her current state brought her much sadness.

★ ★ ★

Utah Reflections

I can count the generations of my family in the Mormon Church back to Joseph Smith and the origins of Mormonism—a continuous and connected whole. Then I count forward again until I get to me. This is where it stops. I've left the church, and I've chosen not to have children—no legacy to pass on and no one to pass it on to. Although both of those decisions are right for me, I can't help feeling as if I've broken an essential connection. I never placed a grandchild into my mother's outstretched hands; we never stood apart, linked by the hands of a toddler between us. We never sat shoulder to shoulder in a church pew, hands entwined, mother and grandmother weeping proudly for the small child encircled by the men who would offer the gift of the Holy Ghost and a lifetime membership.

Over the years, I've searched for the peace and faith in the Mormon Church that the women before me carried with confidence. But I never found it. At age eight, two men lowered me into a warm pool of blue water to cleanse me of whatever sins my small soul might have accumulated thus far. The following day, four men rested their heavy hands on top of my small head to confirm my admission into the Church of Jesus Christ of Latter-Day Saints. After that moment, I stuck close to the women in my family, seeking clarification and understanding of my position in this patriarchal society. But fifty years later, I can still feel the uncomfortable weight of those eight hands on my head every time I enter a Mormon Church. I left the church simply because the presence of men there was stronger than the presence of God.

As a child, I trailed my mother around the house, watching busy hands at eye level scribble out grocery lists, swipe dust off tabletops and polish houseplant leaves. I was attached to her—often literally—clinging to a leg and reaching for those hands. I try now to visualize her young hands, but I cannot conjure up an image, only a sense of touch. I can feel the cool smoothness of my mother's fingers on the side of my face when she kissed me goodnight; I can feel the strength of my mother's hands in my hair as she twisted it into a ponytail; and I can feel the heat of her hands on my back when she pulled me toward her time after time to let me know that my father's wrath could not penetrate that hold. But when I try to *see* her hands, I can see only my own.

In first grade, I loved finger-painting; I loved the visual and tactile sensuality of the paint. Maybe I knew then that I would outlive fluidly moving fingers, that the pleasure of touch would turn to pain. I feel as if I should have better prepared myself for this day, as if I should have braided my hair, opened all jars in the house and photocopied a grocery list I could use in perpetuity so as not to force a pen into my aching hands.

But curling fingers never stopped the Hatch women from writing. They may have winced in pain as they scrawled words on paper, but I place my faith in the stacks of poetry, letters, stories and genealogy occupying boxes in my basement, all written in the same scratched-out scribble of Ethel Gooch Hatch and her daughters.

I often riffle through the papers, feeling the weight of those stories in my hands. I make notes on a pad, not knowing where the notes will lead but hoping they will lead to answers for which the questions have yet to form. I have been at this for years. The beginning notes are neat and legible, written in a sure hand. The notes written yesterday are less so, the lines crooked, the hand less confident.

Before my mother died, we dug through the boxes—then stored in her basement—together. During that time, we clung to each other as if we knew we were coming to the end of something. With my decisions, I have ensured that what she and I shared—a connection that engulfs the love, strength and sacrifice of six generations of Mormon women—will not be repeated. Lately, this does not sit well with me, but I'm not sure why. I am not longing for the child that never was, nor am I entertaining the idea of returning to the Church. I have 32 first cousins—none of whom have left the church—with more than 240 offspring; there is little possibility that the Hatch/Gooch legacy will die out.

What I'm feeling is much closer. It resides within and between my mother and me. I am the beneficiary of the collective gifts—along with the limitations—of these women. Does that not carry with it some sort of obligation? To share, to pass along, to continue? Does it matter that I will cause a break in the chain?

As with my search for faith in the church, which I expected would present itself if given enough opportunity, so went my search for faith in motherhood. The two—motherhood and Mormonism—were inextricably linked in my mind. I had no model for one without the other. I don't know that I ever made a conscious decision not to have children. Instead, I waited patiently for the compelling reason to bring forth a child to clearly emerge from the amalgamation of fear, sadness and anxiety that took occupancy of every small, empty space around me (this, also, an inheritance from the Hatch women). It never did. But now, since burying my mother, I am starkly aware that a piece of myself lies buried, a piece that can be accessed only through motherhood, a piece I will never know.

Yet, in many ways, it was this state of barrenness that gave room to the union between my mother and me. Had we turned our attention to a child in the middle stages of our relationship, would we have dug as deeply into each other? Would we have spent those many hours walking arm in arm through the gardens of the Mormon Temple grounds, our heads tipped toward each other, our voices whispering those things we told no other person? Had I not left the church, had I not been searching for my reasons, would my mother and I have explored our shared history with such passion? Would I have learned that she, too, made unconscious choices from whence there was no return?

Ultimately, it was my mother's love and the cumulative fortitude of the women who came before me that gave me the courage to walk away from my historical legacy of Mormonism and motherhood. But there is sadness in this paradox; it tugs at me when I remember the feel of my mother's hand in mine.

* * *

In the rest home, when Grandmother could no longer lift her curled hand from the bed covers, she cried and pleaded with God to take her. One evening, her children gathered. The four Hatch men linked their straight hands with the already curling hands of the four Hatch women and asked God to take their mother. They fasted and prayed until she died two days later.

When I first began to feel the pain in my thumbs and realized I would have the curled fingers of the Hatch women, I was horrified. But now, when I look at my crippled hands, I am reminded of the things the Hatch women have given me: compassion, perseverance, unyielding strength, a peaceful spirit, a propensity to cry at every occasion and a sense of humor to deal with my curling fingers.

My mother knew she would die before age eighty. Just a feeling, she said. She died seventy days before her eightieth birthday. As her organs began to shut down, I sat next to her bed and stroked her curled fingers with my own.

Chapter 6

THE PRAYER HOLE

by J. Scott Hale

I almost fall while descending the weedy gully to the banks of Parley's Creek. It's where I go to lose myself in thought and find myself in feelings. A refuge. I discovered this place fly-fishing a few years ago, a bend on the creek made deep by a beaver dam. Willows hang down the sides of the gully, and tree branches hang above. Only by kneeling in the middle of the streambed can the most humble of anglers find enough space to cast without losing a fly in the growth overhead. I call it the Prayer Hole.

Though I have enjoyed catching fish and wading these clear waters, I return time and again without rod or line. I am drawn by the sights and sounds of water in motion. It changes with each bend, a place for each of my moods. A small waterfall or rushing riffle. The flat water on one of the many beaver ponds.

The creek chases through a gully bordered by the scrub-oak hillsides of the Wasatch Mountains to the north and a golf course to the south. In the depths of the gully, the sound of water surrounds me.

The Prayer Hole is surrounded by lofty trees that grow along the banks, immovable, protecting this haven from the gaze of passing hikers or the errant ball of a golfer. A fallen tree provides a chair near the bank. I sit, watch and listen. Sheltered by my guardians, the soothing flow before me, I rest, wait to see. Water gurgles through the Prayer Hole, a riffle above, slows and flows toward the beaver dam. The surface reflects myself back to me.

The current tidies the bed of the creek, orange-red stones like pot shards. The native Bonneville Cutthroat trout rise to the surface, shy cheeks blushing red, chasing a passing mayfly or unfortunate beetle. If they see me, they shoot away like armed torpedoes toward hidden targets beneath the undercut banks. Once I slithered on my belly to the edge just above the rising fish, hoping for an uninterrupted peek, when up popped a field mouse, inches from my arm. I startled and alerted the fish. They shot away.

Although they mostly flee from me, I think these fish enjoy my company while I sit at the Prayer Hole. As evening comes, they entertain me. After their initial dash, the trout return to feast in front of me. Birds sing, and a bat gives me a gleeful stunt show.

Other creatures lurk in these woods. A cow moose leaves her footprints, but she remains concealed until I have forgotten about anything such as a moose. Then suddenly, she surprises me before vanishing into the willows.

The beaver are even more elusive. Along Parley's Creek, their fine constructions of sticks and branches are carefully engineered. Yet in all my visits, I have not seen a single beaver. I once found a tall tree with a diameter of two feet chomped halfway through. How many more nights would it take for the beaver to finish the job?

The elusive beer drinker leaves a scattering of aluminum cans on the banks of the creek. Even more mystifying is a rare bird that lays her eggs in flight, the round white eggs marked "Top Flight 3" or "Titleist." I can tolerate the stray ball of a frustrated golfer, but the aluminum, plastic and paper some carelessly leave behind shows disregard for the sanctity of the land. The native animals of these woods prune and care for the garden they are given, and a human foot stomps indifferently on its flowers.

The smooth water of the Prayer Hole is a window. At different times of day, the light passes directly through, revealing every underwater motion of fish or drowned leaf. Hours later, a bright reflection conceals the contents of the stream. The seasons of my life are similar; as water flows, sometimes I comprehend clearly the events carried past. At other times, all I see is a glare, and I am left to guess. Then I must wait for the passing cloud. A slight change of light yields a glimpse of understanding from below the surface. The cloud moves on, and the blinding glare returns. But the memory of the fleeting vision provides enough hope to wait for the next change of light. The veil will lift from the surface of the water. More understanding will come.

I watch my shy friends rise to their tiny prey and fall slowly back into the current. Do they understand how close I am and how long I have been watching? I stand to leave. As I walk upstream a little farther, my body runs cold. I have seen many dead deer while hiking before but not like this one.

Its fur is beautiful and shiny, but its bones are stained with blood, red flesh still clinging to them. Instinctively, I survey my surroundings, looking for the creature that won this prey. I become aware that I am not the only watcher in this forest.

Before long, life's changes will take me away from this place. As I approach the Prayer Hole for the last time, an upstream wind pushes at my back to hurry me along. I sit for a long while before the passing water, oblivious to its reflections, concentrating on the chirping of birds. A sharp splash draws me back to the trout, and I try to appease their jealousy by reassuring them that I'm paying attention.

The evening light fades, and the Prayer Hole is transformed. As the surrounding woods grow darker, the mirror of water stands out brighter, gathering the light. The half moon above softly sings a hymn. The first star joins in, and one by one, more shining voices are heard. The choir broadens and grows. The light from above cuts through the window on the Prayer Hole, not casting a dull glare nor revealing what's under the water. Instead, it pierces through to reveal a whole universe of stars. I look into the water and see stars forever. I view the art of a great sculptor who works in clay, wood and earthen materials. All creations are given life, the sandstone of the creek bed, the fish, the moose and the guardian trees. I see enough light on this night to give me hope for great things to come.

The hymn deepens and fills the night air. Though I now see stars forever, tomorrow the glare on the water will conceal this present view. It is enough to know that I have seen it and that it will reappear again on another night. I leave under the light of the moon and stars with an increased appreciation and understanding. One day, I will return to see the motion of water, visit my shy friends and look deep into the window of the Prayer Hole.

Chapter 7

BALD EAGLES

by Terry Tempest Williams

Lake level: 4211.10′

Rooted. Brooke and I have moved to Emigration Canyon Road, right smack on the trail that Brigham Young and the Latter-Day Saints walked down on their way into the Salt Lake Valley.

We planted four Colorado blue spruces today. Housewarming gifts from Mother and Dad. I held the root ball of each tree and blessed them in this supple soil (so unusual for a wintry day), that they might become the guardians of our home.

Dad and Brooke waited impatiently as they leaned on their shovels.

"I'm sorry, Brooke," Dad said. "All this hocus-pocus did not come from me."

I looked at my father as I stood up and clapped the dirt from my hands. "Who are you kidding, Dad? You are the man who taught us as children about divining for water with sticks, taking us out to a job where you had hired a man as a waterwitch to find where the well might be dug."

"Come on, Terry."

"The way I look at it, John," Brooke said. "We're never going to figure it all out, so we might as well acknowledge the intangibles. Who knows, maybe these trees do have souls."

Mormon religion has roots firmly planted in a magical worldview. Divining rods, seer stones, astrology and visions were all part of the experience of the founding Prophet, Joseph Smith.

Dowsing was viewed negatively by some clergymen, "not because it leads to treasure, but because it leads to information." Divining rods were understood by many to be instruments of revelation, used not just to locate veins of water or minerals but to shepherd answers to questions. In folk magic, a nod up meant yes, a lack of movement meant no. Joseph Smith was not only familiar with this tradition, he and his family were practitioners of it—along with the use of seer stones, which they used for treasure seeking.

Critics of Mormonism have used this to cast doubt on the origins and faith of this American religion. They dismiss Joseph Smith's discovery of "the golden plates" buried near Palmyra, New York—which contained the holy doctrine translated in the Book of Mormon—as simply an extension of the treasure-hunting days of his youth.

Others claim that Smith's sensitivity to matters of the occult heightened his shamanistic gifts and contributed to his developing spirituality.

For me, it renders my religion human. I love knowing that Joseph Smith was a mystic who ascribed magical properties to animals and married his wives according to the astrological "mansions of the moon."

To acknowledge that which we cannot see, to give definition to that which we do not know, to create divine order out of chaos is the religious dance.

I have been raised in a culture that believes in personal revelation, that it is not something buried and lost with ancient prophets of the Old Testament. In the early days of the Mormon Church, authority was found within the individual, not outside.

In 1971, when Mother was diagnosed with breast cancer, the doctors said she had less than a 20 percent chance of surviving two years. Mother did not know this. Dad did. I found out only because I overheard the conversation between my father and the doctors.

Months passed. Mother was healing. It was stake conference, a regional gathering of church members that meets four times a year. My father was a member of the stake high council, a group of high priests who direct the membership on both organizational and spiritual matters. President Thomas S. Monson, one of the Twelve Apostles, directly beneath the Prophet, who at that time was Joseph Fielding Smith, was conducting interviews for the position of stake president.

Before conference, President Monson met with my father privately, as he did with all councilmen. He asked him, if called, would he serve as stake president? My father's reply was no. In a religion that believes all leadership positions are decided by God, this was an unorthodox response.

"Brother Tempest, would you like to explain?"

My father simply said it would be inappropriate to spend time away from his wife when she had so little time left.

President Monson stood and said, "You are a man whose priorities are intact."

After conference, my father was returning to his car. He heard his name called, ignored it at first, until he heard it for a second time. He turned to find President Monson, who put his hand on Dad's shoulder.

"Brother Tempest, I feel compelled to tell you your wife will be well for many years to come. I would like to invite you and your family to kneel together in the privacy of your home at noon on Thursday. The Brethren will be meeting in the holy chambers of the temple, where we will enter your wife's name among those to be healed."

Back home, our family was seated around the dinner table. Dad was late. Mother was furious. I'll never forget the look on his face when he opened the door. He walked over to Mother and held her tightly in his arms. He wept.

"What's happened, John?" Mother asked.

That Thursday, my brothers and I came home from school to pray. We knelt in the living room together as a family. No words were uttered. But in the quiet of that room, I felt the presence of angels.

"What would you have me know?" I asked. "Faith," my great-grandmother Vilate said to me. Mother and my grandmother Lettie and I were helping to pack up her apartment. She was moving to a retirement center. "Faith, my child. It is the first and sweetest principle of the gospel."

At the time, I did not appreciate her answer. Faith, to a college coed, was a denouncement of knowledge, a passive act more akin to resignation than resolve.

"Where would faith in the Vietnam War have gotten us? Or faith in the preservation of endangered species without legislation?" I argued.

"My darling, faith without works is dead."

That is all I remember of our discussion. But today, the idea of faith returns to me. Faith defies logic and propels us beyond hope because it is not attached to our desires. Faith is the centerpiece of a connected life. It allows us to live by the grace of invisible strands. It is a belief in a wisdom superior to our own. Faith becomes a teacher in the absence of fact.

The four trees we planted will grow in the absence of my mother. Faith holds their roots, the roots I can no longer see.

"I can't believe this is my body," Mother said as she looked in the mirror of the dressing room at Nordstrom's. "I could never have imagined myself this thin...and these scars..." She shuddered.

I took the red suede chemise, size 6, off the padded hanger and handed it to her. She stepped into the dress and put one arm in, then the other, then buttoned the front and turned the collar up.

"It's perfect, isn't it?" she said, turning sideways to see how it hung in the back.

"Perfect," I replied. "You look absolutely beautiful."

She turned to me, her eyes radiant. "Right now, at this moment, I can honestly tell you, I feel wonderful! John will love this, even if it is extravagant."

She gave me back the dress. "I'll take it," she said, quickly putting on her black skirt and sweater. I held her emerald green jacket behind her as she slipped her arms through.

"Thank you," she said as she picked up her purse. "Shall we move on to our Christmas list?"

The rest of the day was spent in a shopping frenzy: three Christian Dior nightgowns for aunts; a shirt and tie for Steve; a reindeer sweater for Brooke; books for Dan; guitar strings for Hank; a ceramic crèche for Ann; a silver vase for a niece; pistachios for neighbors; a dozen narcissus bulbs; a pair of black patent-leather pumps to go with her new red dress; and two Madame Alexander dolls for her granddaughters, Callie and Sara.

Waiting for all the packages to be wrapped, she stood while I sat. Mother's energy and quick pace was back. I followed three steps behind.

We had lunch at Hotel Utah: poached salmon. We laughed and chatted over absolute trivia.

"Let's make this an annual affair," Mother said.

We both believed it.

By the time we picked up our packages, it was late afternoon. I drove her home. As she got out of the car, she screamed, "Oh, Terry, look!"

The sun was a scarlet ball shimmering above the lake. Mother put down her shopping bags and applauded.

"How much should I tell her?" Dr. Smith asked me in his office. Mother was in the examining room.

"Tell her the truth," I said. "As you have always done." I could feel the tears well up in my eyes. I was trying to be brave.

"You can't be surprised, Terry. I thought you had accepted this last summer."

"We did. I mean, I had, but hope can be more powerful and deceptive than love."

"Her weight loss of eight more pounds is not a result of flu. It's the cancer. She doesn't have much time," he said. He walked out and opened the door to Mother's room.

After the examination, he came back out and said things looked better than he thought, that the tumor he had felt in June was gone and that the others felt smaller.

Mother was very quiet. On the way home, I asked, "What do you think?"

"It doesn't really matter, does it?" she said. "Let's just take one day at a time."

I had the sense that she wanted to cry. And I thought of her mother, how once in the nursing home, after we had been crying together, I said, "Oh, Grandmother, doesn't it feel good to cry?" and she replied, "Only if you know there is an end to your tears."

Mother and I returned to my new house in the canyon. I fixed some chamomile tea.

"This tastes so good," she said with her hands cupped around the mug. "I can't seem to keep warm."

Mother asked for some more tea. We both settled on the couch. I gave her a mohair shawl to wrap around her shoulders.

"I think I have denied having cancer for years. It's a survival skill. You put it out of your mind and you get on with your life." She paused. "I mean, you have momentary flashes of what is real in periods of crisis and you face them, but then your mind seems to leap over the illness. You forget you were ever sick, much less that you are living with a life-threatening disease. The curious thing in all of this is that I have never acknowledged my anger over losing my breast as a young woman. Isn't that strange? Why would that come up now, after almost sixteen years? I'm angry, Terry."

Mother broke down. We both cried.

"I guess I'm giving up all sense of who I am," she said. "Last month, when John and I were at the beach in Laguna, all I could do was stare out at the waves."

The lake is frozen. Because of the ice, you can travel farther west—if you dare.

My friend Roz Newmark and I drove out to the Bird Refuge in my trustworthy station wagon—as far as we could, until the lake stopped us.

It was a dreamscape where the will of the land overtakes you. I felt as though we were standing under the wing of a great blue heron.

As we walked, each step brought about a wheezing from the ice. The ice was thin, showing asphalt below. Off the road, it was a magnifying glass for objects arrested in motion. A floating feather—when was it caught in the clamps of ice? The quill tapered off, bleeding into darkness.

Stories from the Wasatch Front

The banks of Great Salt Lake in winter. *Photo credit Jason Chacon.*

The ice became thinner and thinner until each step of our boots sounded like vertebrae popping. We stopped. Beneath the icy veneer was a stream of suspended detritus: two snail shells, root fragments and reeds, a Canada goose feather, down, burrs, a piece of Styrofoam, a small hollowed corncob, pebbles, decaying insects, fish bones, carp scales, a woman's shoe.

Farther out, the ice looked solid. It was milky and dense. Roz and I dared each other to go first. Finally, we took hold of each other's gloved hands and began skating away from the road. I held my breath, as though it would make us lighter.

We lasted until moans, groans and squeaks of the ice sent us back in a hurry. Roz, a dancer by profession, had an enormous advantage as she threw her head back, swung her arms in the air and leaped across the ice. I settled for short shuffles. Back on the road, we swung each other western-style, joyous in our bravado.

We wandered a mile or two west, still on the same road. Two ravens flew across, their caws like chatter in a cathedral. The quiet returned. Twelve bald eagles stood on the ice of Great Salt Lake, looking like white-hooded monks. From November through March, they grace northern Utah. When the ice disappears, so do they.

Eagles on ice, cleaning up carp: beak to flesh. Flesh to bone. They whittle carrion down to a sculpture, exhibited in a bleak and lonely landscape.

Ice can immobilize, but on Great Salt Lake, it creates habitat. I pluck the edge of the ice—it rings with the character of crystal. Ice that supports eagles is of the finest quality.

Where the Bear River bends and flows south, the eagles flew. They appeared as a small thought against the Wasatch Range.

Roz was sitting on her heels, wondering how life goes on in the river beneath the ice. Taking off her gloves, she ran her hand back and forth across its surface. Trapped bubbles, resembling clusters of fish eggs, were a reminder that fish swam below.

"It is comforting to know this," she said.

Mother was dead. I sat up, startled, and leaned against the pine headboard of our bed. Mother was alive. I wrapped my arms around myself to stop shaking from the nightmare.

But the feeling I could not purge from my soul was that without a mother, one no longer has the luxury of being a child.

I have never felt so alone.

December 16, 1986. Mother and I made a pact that we would no longer discuss how she was feeling physically, unless she wanted to.

"Good," she said. "So what do you have going on today?"

"Grading papers for my class on 'Women and Nature' at the university," I said. "And I've got a few things to take care of at the museum. What about you?"

"John and I have the annual Church Christmas Ball at Hotel Utah tonight."

"Are you excited about going?" I asked.

"Very."

"Your red dress?"

"My red dress," she answered.

I saw Mother asking my father to dance before anyone dared step onto the parquet floor.

Chapter 8

FEBRUARY 14

by Katharine Coles

This morning, a house finch sings and bounces
Its bare branch outside our window

Though the sky falls, though snow
Covers the ground. Under the snow

Crocuses swell and the Lenten rose
Already waxes. Our penance

Has yet to begin, our last pulling
Back to eke out meager stores

While we tick off our wrongs. Today,
An old saint signs himself

Yours before losing his head.
And so. Do we

Need an excuse? Our patience
Already ended. Outside,

My husband shovels snow from flower beds
Back onto the drive. Today the birds

Utah Reflections

The Wasatch Mountains blanketed by a thick winter storm. *Photo credit Jason Chacon.*

Begin mating, I once was told,
Their clear sense of things

Tocking them. This
Little finch, not yet come

Into his plumage, sings
Everything could happen. Wily, every poem

Hatches its little lie. Time changes. Just
Between us, how I like it.

Chapter 9

THE WASATCH FRONT AND BACK

by Stevan Allred

average annual rainfall, Sanpete County, Utah: sixteen inches
average annual rainfall, Emery County, Utah: eight inches
average annual rainfall, Portland, Oregon: more than forty inches

If you asked my grandfather about the mountains of Emery County, on the back side of the Wasatch Front, he would raise his leathery farmer's face in their direction. "They're beautiful," he would say, and they certainly were, shaped by wind and rain and erosion into crenellated turrets and walled fortresses, into a forbidding kind of beauty. But there was something sad and broken about the way my grandfather looked at those weathered heights, as if living in the shadow of their beauty came at a high price.

My family's roots straddled the Wasatch Range 130 years ago. In the summer of 1884, my great-great-grandfather Wiley Payne Allred moved his family from Spring City in Sanpete County to a dugout on the banks of the Muddy, a turbid creek in Emery County. Emery County lay to the east of Sanpete, on the other side of the Wasatch Range. Wiley Payne had sons who needed land, and he answered a call from the Mormon prophet Brigham Young to settle land outside the Wasatch Front. What they found in Emery County was alkaline soil and a climate noticeably harsher than the valley of the Great Salt Lake. My great-grandfather Isaac, fourteen at the time of the move, thought the land "lonely and desolate and mostly inhabited with coyotes and prairie dogs."

Utah Reflections

Drinking water in the desert of Emery County. *Photo credit Emery County Archives.*

They had moved from twenty acres of good tillable ground with a family orchard, and a house built of rock, to the dugout, which was little more than a wide trench cut into the bank of the Muddy, roofed over with timbers and the timbers covered with dirt. They'd gone from wood floors to dirt floors and from a solid roof to something that leaked in a heavy rain. They settled along the Muddy for the water, but the waters of the Muddy were a disappointment, for the irrigable farmland the Muddy allowed was scant.

There were hundreds of acres of flat land to the south and west, but to farm there, the settlers would have to divert the Muddy on the eastern slope of the Wasatch Range and move themselves some eight miles to the present site of the town of Emery. To farm there, the settlers had to build a canal eleven miles long to bring water down from the mountains, and they dug that canal by hand. This canal ran at one point through a 1,200-foot-long tunnel. They dug that tunnel by hand.

"When the water was turned into the canal," my great-grandfather Isaac wrote, "the people were very jubilant." But the tunnel soon suffered a series of cave-ins, cutting off the supply of water to the new farms of Emery, and the men had to repeatedly clear the cave-ins, again by hand. Great-grandfather Isaac, who would have been seventeen or eighteen at the time, was sent into the tunnel with another man to clear a large cave-in. They worked until mid-afternoon and then took a break to eat lunch. When they returned to the site of the cave-in, a two-ton rock had fallen on the very spot where they were working.

The people decided they must cut timbers and shore up the walls and ceiling of the tunnel for the entire length. The timbering of the tunnel took several more months of hard labor, the men braving more cave-ins as they worked.

That's how important water is.

When I was a boy growing up in the rainy Pacific Northwest city of Seattle, I used to visit Emery in the summertime, staying with my grandparents in their home, which they had built of adobe bricks they made themselves and covered with stucco. I thought Emery was the back of beyond, and I was not far from the truth, for if the Wasatch Front has a Wasatch Back, Emery would be dead center in it. On the other side of the mountains that Emery was backed up against were the towns my cousins lived in—American Fork, Orem, Pleasant Grove—towns where there were green parks and movie theaters and kids to play with. Emery, for an eight-year-old boy whose only company was his sixty-three-year-old grandparents, was pretty damn desolate.

My grandfather must have thought so, too. Cattle farming in Emery was hard, the feed being so poor in the high desert. It meant moving the cattle into the mountain meadows for summer grazing and feeding them alfalfa hay in the winters. The size of a farmer's herd was determined by his grazing permit and how much alfalfa he could grow with the water diverted from the Muddy.

When my grandfather came back from World War I to Emery, he married my grandmother and started a family. He had married a woman who wanted something more than what life in Emery afforded, and so he took a job in a coal mine for five dollars a day. The work was dangerous—men died in those mines—but the pay was regular, and mine work was the only hope my grandfather had to make enough money to move his family to the more hospitable Wasatch Front. He saved enough money working in the mines to put a down payment on a house and five acres on the edge of Salt Lake City. He had the promise of a job at the post office if he moved. He moved his family to Salt Lake City in the late 1920s.

The farm in Emery was put up for sale, but there were no takers. In Salt Lake City, the family planted a garden, and they raised chickens and sold eggs and eked out a living. Then came October 1929, when the stock market crashed and the Great Depression began. The job at the post office never materialized. My grandfather, having failed to find a secure foothold on the Wasatch Front, retreated to the Wasatch Back and the high desert farm he had hoped to leave behind.

My grandparents spent the rest of their productive lives on that farm, barely scraping by though they worked hard. My grandfather went back to the coal mines, leaving my father and his older brother to run the farm by themselves during the week, and he came home on weekends to farm and go to church with his family on Sundays. The blow to the dreams of their youth shaped my grandparents into the people I knew as a boy. My grandfather was a silent man and a stoic. My grandmother flitted about nervously, birdlike, anxious. They gave their faith, unshaken it seems, to God and the church authorities, and they found comfort in the bonds of family. Desert farming had made my grandparents tough, but the Great Depression had made them wary, and they both had the habit of staring, their wrinkled, sun-beaten faces scanning some interior middle distance, watching for trouble.

It took my family three generations to find their way back to the Wasatch Front. Three generations of scraping a living from that alkaline soil, of building fences out of ragged branches scavenged from the foothills, of looking at that cloudless blue sky and praying for rain.

My father was born on the last day of 1925, the third of seven children. He came of age during World War II, and in 1944, he enlisted in the navy, serving as a signalman on a supply ship in the Pacific. He married my mother while he was home on leave in December 1944, just before he shipped out. When his navy hitch was over, he went to Utah State College in Logan on the GI Bill and then on to a master's in social work at the University of Washington. "I used to have to get up every morning in the dark to do chores," he told me. "I liked sociology a lot better." He spent his working life as a social worker and therapist, first in Seattle and then in Portland.

His sisters married men who found work as plumbers and doctors and dentists in the towns of the Wasatch Front. His younger brother became a supplier of HVAC equipment and ended up owning his own business. One sister married a mine manager who lived in Price, just north of Emery County, but their lives were urban, housing development sort of lives and had nothing to do with farming. Only his older brother stayed in agriculture. He became a dry land farmer in eastern Washington, in country with no more rainfall than Emery County but with a lot more irrigation water available.

None of my father's siblings stayed in Emery County.

My mother's people settled in Ferron, fifteen miles to the northwest of Emery. What I know of the town of Ferron is only what my mother told me, and what she told me was that her childhood was happy. Her father was a kind and loving man who grew the best peaches in Emery County. They were cash poor, like all of their neighbors, but they had food to eat, and what they couldn't afford to buy they made do without. Every spring, the whole town turned out to drive their cattle up into the mountain meadows where they would spend the summer grazing. They camped out at Ferron reservoir for a few days, working together to get the cattle and the men who would stay with them situated for the summer and having a town party while they did it.

These towns still exist, although Emery (current population 308) is listed as a semi–ghost town on one map. Ferron has long been a somewhat larger town (current population 1,626) and went through a population boom in the '80s when two coal-fired electrical generation plants were built in nearby Castle Dale and Huntington.

My mother's people abandoned Emery County for Los Angeles during and after World War II. They moved there for jobs in the defense industry and the surrounding economy. Like my father's family, they found that the dry, alkaline land of Emery County would not support the next generation, and so they left the Wasatch Back because leaving was the only way to go forward.

My parents moved us to a house and five acres on the edge of Beaverton, a suburb of Portland, Oregon, in 1962. The five acres was a pasture, and the grass was waist high. I kept a flock of sheep on that pasture, and we raised cattle. My older brother kept bees, a rather odd thing to do for a high school boy in suburban Portland in 1961, but we had roots in agriculture, and we did these things because our parents encouraged us to and because it was part of our family culture. We kept a large vegetable garden, fertilized by mounds of cow manure we hauled each spring from our cowshed and tilled into the soil.

When my grandfather came to visit from Emery, he stood in that pasture and marveled at how many cattle we could feed on five acres. He was near the end of his farming life and too old to start over someplace new. He was there to hand on something to my father, his blessing, perhaps, and his recognition that his son had found fertile ground with more than adequate rainfall. If another Great Depression came, we would not starve.

In the rainy Pacific Northwest, in what we might call, given the terms of this essay, the Cascade Front, forty or more inches of rain means a lot of dark and drizzly days from November to May and sometimes on into July. But it also means a garden with so much zucchini you can't give it all away. It means cucumbers by the bushel and tomatoes so juicy they squirt all the way across a picnic table when you bite into them.

In 1980, I bought my first home on a rural road outside Oregon City, less than five miles from where the Oregon Trail ended. The house was a split-entry ranch-style house on three acres. I was living a countercultural life, had hair down to the middle of my back and had long since left the Mormon Church behind. I was pretty alienated from my parents, in ways that now seem trivial and almost quaint, and would remain so until I started a family of my own. (After my first son was born, the idea of grandparents took on a whole new meaning.) But I remember clearly the morning that I went down my driveway to get the mail and, walking back to the house, took a moment to look at my new home.

What I saw was a conventional mid-'70s house with a yard and a big picture window looking out from the living room. I had gone to a lot of effort to make of myself someone completely different from my parents, but now I saw that I had gone out and bought a house just like theirs. I had a large garden, just like theirs, even though I had hated gardening as a boy. And it came to me that my parents' house was a direct descendant of the house and five acres my grandfather bought on the edge of Salt Lake City just before the crash of 1929.

Except that we had plenty of water. I had a spring-fed year-round stream running in the gully next to the driveway and a spring dribbling water into a perpetually soggy spot in my yard. My parents had a stream at the bottom of their pasture, and their pasture flooded every winter when the rains came, standing water three feet deep at times.

All of us—my grandfather, my father, myself—loved the dry desert beauty of Emery County. My mother's people felt the same way. But the harshness of farm life in Emery County, in the heart of the Wasatch Back, had marked us. The bitter lessons of my grandfather's failed move to the Wasatch Front were internalized for the next two generations. The future is never certain. Water, or the lack of it, will determine who stays on the land and who must move on to prosper. Prosperity, if it was to be had at all, must be found on the front side of things and not in the back of beyond.

And prosperity is so much easier to get if you have a little rain.

Chapter 10
GEOGRAPHIES OF HOME

by Jen Henderson

On a metal bulletin board over my desk, I've pinned two postcards, both aerial views of geographies as diverse as the cultures they represent. In one, a curved sickle of beach bisects the azure water of the Atlantic Ocean from the row of houses and inland waters of Topsail Island, North Carolina. It's where my husband, Dane, and I have vacationed each Thanksgiving since we moved to Virginia almost nine years ago. In the other, the snow-tipped peaks of the Wasatch Front in Utah ring the valley of my ancestors, Mormon pioneers who came to the state of Deseret in search of religious autonomy. I escape to the former and walk the wide beaches morning and evening, letting the relentless tide remind me of my insignificance in the world. I return to the other to remember why I matter and, more importantly, to whom.

I moved from my childhood home in 1999 when I followed my then boyfriend, now husband, to graduate school in Pullman, Washington, a landscape with agricultural fields that swell and crest in emerald wheat. I used to tell my family I could never live in Utah again. "It's too claustrophobic," I'd say. Former lovers, lapsed religious beliefs, family complications—these all felt overwhelming, a kind of baggage we were unwilling to carry across such routine ground.

Now, I'm wondering if I'm not ready to go back.

This instinct to return to Utah intensifies with each conversation I have with my mom, descendant of German, Scottish and Irish immigrants, daughter of poverty and resilience. The youngest of thirteen children, Mom represents the last of her generation. She has begun a slow descent into what we fear is dementia, a family affliction it would seem. Memory loss plagues her older sister; her brother, who died just a few months ago; and her mother, whose senility took her quickly when I was a little girl.

A few times each week, we talk on the phone. I imagine her sitting in her home in Ogden, a nine-hundred-square-foot bungalow, with her husband, Charlie. She talks about how she's ready to retire, how she'd like the last years of her memory to be freed from the concerns of a job she's held for over twenty years. And she wants her grandchildren to know her better. She whispers, "I can't believe this is happening to me. It doesn't seem like it's me but someone else, like I'm watching from outside myself."

I listen and try to reassure her. I tell her that she's not alone and that we all hate this for her.

"I think I deserve a break," she says, returning to thoughts of retirement. I tell her I agree. She raised four children, cared for aunts and uncles, her own parents and my dad's folks, and now at a youthful sixty-one, she would like to take time for herself. Whatever shape that self might eventually become.

I vaguely remember her own mother at this age, Margarite Martha Bessan—Grandma Andrus—daughter of Lewis Christian Bessan, second-generation Utahn, and Ottilie Zacher, a Prussian immigrant and Mormon convert. She came to live with us for a few weeks when she was in her sixties, hunched over with osteoporosis. I recall that even at this age, her thick hair curled in black whorls, a contrast to the Henderson gene I inherited, all angel fine wisps in muted brown. Grandma had lived through two husbands, the first a panhandler for gold who made her and their five children live out of their car; the second, a womanizer who went a little crazy after he was buried up to his neck in coal when he worked at Kennecott mine, or the story goes. She cared for him as his health declined, until her own suffered, as well.

During one of our conversations, I read to my mom excerpts about her paternal grandmother, Christine Eliza Rider. One entry recorded in a journal by a cousin says, "Every Saturday [Grandma] dressed up and took the bus to Salt Lake City and met her friends or family for lunch and shopping. Every afternoon she would take a nap. Though her life was difficult at times she decided instead of crying she would laugh. This is what my children remembered most about her."

Mom listens quietly.

The Andrus family. *Photo credit Jen Henderson.*

"I wonder," she says when I finish, "what will you all remember most about me?"

My voice catches in my throat as I try not to break down. *So much*, I want to say. Her kindness with her elderly friends, her love of animals, her way of slightly altering words so that *disoriented* becomes *disorientated*, *Alzheimer's* becomes *Alheimer's*. I will remember her soft voice and the way she sucks in her stomach in front of mirrors, hoping that the "pooch" below her navel will be disguised by jeans. I'll remember her crazy diets from when we were kids, like the one composed only of hot dogs and water, and how she will stop in a rainstorm and offer her umbrella and coat to a perfect stranger. And I'll remember her stories.

Before I can recount the list, however, she laughs. "Don't worry. You won't have to remember me. I'm going to live forever."

She tells me, as she always does, how she knows that we all—she and her children—were angels "on the other side" in heaven. "We were best friends, and we had to decide who would be the mother and who would be the children." She volunteered to come first. "I've never wanted to be anything other than your mom."

"I know," I say. "And you're so good at it." We both start to cry.

This is what draws me back, the blend of land and people, culture and religion that have shaped the contours of my family history. A homeland, writes geographer David Sopher, "is not material landscape but people... It is one's relations with this nurturing and sheltering group as they are associated with the landscape that give it meaning as the landscape of home." Perhaps this explains why other places I've lived have continued to fade in the way they register in my mind and why the sensory elements of aesthetic appreciation have continued but the deeper attachments I once felt pale and soften. Or maybe it's something else.

Over the last year, the western topography alone fills my mind. I smell sagebrush in my herb garden, the scent of arid cool mornings hiking Indian Trail overcoming the humid blue of Virginia. I close my eyes to the shimmer of aspens, the sequins that color morning hikes near our family cabin above Kamas. I hear the hollow sway of lodgepole pines, their serrated tops bowing in the evening breeze near King's Peak in the Uintas. Some days, I even find myself wandering the spines of slot canyons near Escalante, where Dane and I began our relationship. These environments map my past, a projection of parallels and meridians that grid the space of memory. Time is a sphere onto which this map projects, warping the distance between events, obscuring beginnings and endings, a resolution that smoothes the years so that my life appears as a clear and distinct line, however wavy its trajectory.

The first time I chased storms, it was with Dane. We headed out in his Geo Metro, lured by the electrical storm fingering lightning above the Great Salt Lake. We sped along the back roads, both of us in our early twenties,

Stories from the Wasatch Front

The aspen trees speckle the mountains and valleys of the Wasatch Front. *Photo credit Jen Henderson.*

hoping to see something more magnificent than a god in which we no longer believed. Instead, we found ourselves in a field of inky blackness, the brine shrimp of the lake pungent in the air. The two of us sat in silence as bolts of light spread like sparks of static along the dark. I anchored my neck, craning to see through the top of the windshield. Dane glanced out the side of the car into the middle distance where lake and not lake blurred.

Then, a brightness and simultaneous sound so deafening I couldn't hear my own scream, which reverberated across my face. "I can't see!" I yelled. "Dane, are we dead?"

The white light seared into a green-gray afterglow. I reached out my hand and touched his knee. "We're okay," he said faintly. "That was close."

It never occurred to me, to us, that we could be in danger in such a familiar place. I'd seen dozens of storms, a waterspout even, and never questioned my safety. Only later, when I moved to Kansas for graduate school, when I witnessed my first tornado emerging from a pale blister on the underside of a supercell, did I feel threatened by a locale, unknown and strange. Only then did I understand how vulnerability derives from perspective, from distance. In the midst of an intimate setting, it's easy to take life for granted.

Perhaps I've lived long enough away from my home that I can see it more plainly. I see its flaws: the incessant development that has transformed the farms of my youth to suburbia, the inversion that masks the mountains for months in the winter, the undercurrent of tension between faith and reason. Returning to Utah now would mean coming to some angle of repose, unsure, precarious, like leaning into the wind. Ironically, it would mean choosing that which is no longer protected and sure. After all, Utah has changed as much as I have over the past decade. Or perhaps I'm choosing to no longer remain impervious to the elements of my childhood, which for years made me long to be somewhere else.

"Can you imagine if we'd never left?" I'd ask Dane at least a few times a year, usually after one of our yearly visits with family. He'd look at me over the rim of his wire-frame glasses, his blue eyes fixing me: "No."

We felt this way for years, glad we lived somewhere else, anywhere, really. At one point, I would have said the farther the better.

Postcards remind us of vacations we've taken or been privy to. They represent transitory passage, fleeting and romantic. Images selected for these souvenirs frame our perceptions so that we see someone else's view, the desired view, the most scenic or symbolic of the surface of things. Keeping one of the far northeastern edge of the Great Basin, for me, however, is not about visitation or exotic trips abroad. I recognize this topography from all scales, like wrinkles on my face, like veins. Mountains of granite slab forced upward through the skin of terra firma are a compass. They don't lead me back to a place so much as a person, a set of people.

I don't have any children of my own, a deliberate choice, one that Dane and I didn't come to lightly. And sometimes I consider a future without either of us in it. I wonder what it will look like, who will enjoy it, how they will feel about the spatial extent of land that has shaped my life. I wonder what I

Jen Henderson's grandma Joyce and Topaz.
Photo credit Jen Henderson.

might have shared with a son or daughter, what they would revere most about their home.

"You can share me," my eight-year-old niece, Topaz, might say. I'll cup her face in my hands and look over her watercolor features, so much like her grandma's. A wash of pale eyes, freckled skin and blond hair golden with highlights. She looks as though she could be my mother's child. And for that I'm grateful.

In that moment, I'd like to think she and I will walk along a path under the shade of sycamores, the horizon lined with the snowy crests of the Wasatch. Or maybe we'll hike through the woods around our cabin, Topaz pointing out horse tracks, deer scat, what she claims could be the imprint of a bear in mud, and I taking it all in, the both of us losing ourselves to each other amid the chatter of aspens.

Chapter 11

EVAPORATION

by Sylvia Torti

José was in his car on the street when I pulled into my driveway. I think it was summer, though I can't remember for sure. If it was summer, then I know it was hot. My windows would have been rolled up, the air conditioning on just enough to keep my mood in the tempered zone. If it was summer, the Utah sun would have been brilliant and constant, the air dry and brittle, and getting out of my car, I'd feel the familiar absence of trees. I'd look around, squint through my sunglasses and wonder how I ever came to live in an American desert.

I shut the car door, raised my hand toward the street. Though I'd spoken with him on the phone to give him directions, José hadn't yet gotten out of his car, and so I didn't know what he looked like. I also didn't know that his real name wasn't José.

Basins collect things. Water, soil, rocks, bones, anything that follows the laws of gravity. Salt Lake Valley is part of the Great Basin—that "huge heart-shaped" stretch of western landscape formed from slips in the earth's crust, faults along areas of implausible earthly weakness. It's an endorheic basin, which just means water flows in and gets stuck in the low spots. There is no river or stream going downhill. There is no way out. Except, that is, to change form.

My younger sister, who was living in Salt Lake at the time, had called from work. A young Mexican man, who didn't speak English, had shown up at the furniture store looking for a job. She knew I had a bathroom project going on and the sanding was going to take a long while. She

Antelope Island. *Photo credit Sylvia Torti.*

Antelope Island at sunset. *Photo credit Jason Chacon.*

thought I might hire him. My arms were tired, and I was anxious to get back to writing my novel, based on the Zapatista Rebellion of 1994 in Chiapas, Mexico, and so I agreed.

José got out of the car. He wasn't much taller than I but more muscular. His hair was straight and black, his cheekbones broad, his skin dark. We shook hands and introduced ourselves in Spanish, and I remember thinking that his hands were small for a man's. We went into the house. I showed him the work, and he agreed to the job. I gave him an electric sander and a mask and left him in the bathroom, and then I went back down to my basement to write.

Of course, it's only called "the" Great Basin. It's really a multitude of basins, each one collecting its own bit of precipitation, the melted snow that falls each winter and accumulates for a while in the spring. But when the dry heat arrives on the first day of summer, as it does—relentlessly and constantly—evaporation quickly exceeds precipitation. The van der Waal's forces between water molecules are broken, and each molecule is pulled up into the dry air and held in its new form as vapor. We're left with the salts. White salts that form a reflective film over the dry, gray soil.

I'd started writing fiction about Chiapas in 1998, the year before I met José, as a way to process my experience there. I had arrived in Ocosingo, Chiapas, on New Year's Eve 1993, and after a walk through town with some Mexican, Venezuelan and American biologists to buy an old and very tough chicken to grill, I'd gone to bed (a sleeping bag on the tile floor) thinking about bird surveys, coffee plantations and the shady rainforest. We woke before dawn the next morning and prepared to go out and in the foggy morning air, we found not birds but young men with bandanas over their faces, rifles in their hands. During those first days of the Zapatista Rebellion, I'd clung close to what I knew: Latin American history (though sketchy when it came to Mexico), the lilt of the Spanish language and tropical plant identification (*Lantana, Ceiba, Simaruba*). There was the new and unsettling sense to my twenty-four-year-old self that the world could shift at any moment.

Ocosingo is also a basin, just not an endorheic one. Over one hundred inches of rain fall per year. The soil and air are wet because here precipitation exceeds evaporation; rivers flow out and down toward the forest and then the sea. Ocosingo is a lush, green and highly productive valley, which is why cattle farmers took over the land and why indigenous groups were pushed up into the marginal lands on the hills or, worse yet, into the wet rainforest where they didn't know how to make a living. It's a basin that over the millennia has collected species, temples and stories, all hidden below reddish brown soil and broad green leaves.

Novelists collect things too. We collect and then filter consciously and unconsciously before we process and produce on the page. So far in my novel, I'd written a story from the perspective of an American biologist, a woman who understood neither the Spanish language nor Latin culture and who had, prior to arriving in Chiapas, never been out of the United States. I'd written another story from the perspective of an indigenous woman fighting with the Zapatistas. (She came out of glimpses of Zapatistas on the hillside and my own love of trees and the rainforest.) Those two stories, read to fellow writers, grew to four stories as I rounded out the characters to include a male biologist from a prominent Mexican City family (loosely fashioned after an American biologist friend) and a soldier in the Mexican army who was sent to fight the Zapatistas (based on no one I could muster).

I checked in on José an hour later, offered him a glass of water and engaged in a bit of chitchat. His Spanish was hard to understand because his accent was unfamiliar to me and he used words I'd never heard. And perhaps, as I now guess, Spanish was not his first language because in later conversations I learned that he'd grown up in Guerrero, where many people don't speak Spanish.

In an effort to connect, I told him I'd been in Chiapas in 1994 and that I'd been there during the Zapatista Rebellion. To my surprise, he said he'd spent time in Chiapas too. We discussed timelines, and it turned out that he'd arrived just after I'd left. It also turned out that he'd been in the Mexican army and sent to Chiapas to fight the Zapatistas.

So here, in my home, by a strange coincidence, was a man who embodied the rough outline of Mario, the soldier character in my story. What did I do? I did what any writer would do. I started to collect. I asked him questions, lots of questions. What was it like? What did you eat? What did you think then? What did you feel? What do you think now?

When José left my house that first day, he hesitated at the front door, reached into his back pocket and pulled out his wallet. He held two cards in front of me. "José is not my real name," he said. "It's the name on this card, but I want you to know my real name. I don't like to lie to people." I leaned in and took note of the second identity card and his real name.

If you were to ask me now, I could not tell you what name I read. I've forgotten, perhaps never recorded it, but as I said, novelists collect stories. I know that José, the man in my house, whose real name wasn't José, became Mario, born in Guerrero, and Mario spoke in my book.

Utah Reflections

My cousin, Domingo, told me all about it. He's been going for years now, working odd jobs. There's even some rich woman who gives him easy work whenever he wants it. He just shows up at her house, and she asks him to weed the garden or wash the car, and she pays him double what he makes doing anything else.

During the months that followed, José came over a number of times. Sometimes I'd have a job for him, sometimes he'd simply stop by, usually around dinnertime, and we'd set an extra plate on the table and eat together. And then, suddenly, he didn't come anymore. I continued writing, taking what he'd told me about the awful army food, the tough horsemeat, the cold mornings, the utter misery he felt in Chiapas, and worked them into the novel.

A few months later, when there was a ring at the door, José was back at my house. He'd been to Kansas, he said. Working in a chicken factory. He wanted to know if I had a job for him. It was fall, I think, because I remember raking leaves in the front yard together. We chatted in the cool air, and he told me about the chicken farm, the dust, the smell, the midwestern summer heat. He said that after he bought better papers, he could get a better job. He wanted to buy a car with new hubcaps. Something that would shine in the sunlight.

Mario spoke: *Last year he worked on a chicken farm.* "The gringos have huge farms just for chickens," he told me. We laughed hard at that. Everyone knows that the guys who travel across the border are called *pollos*, chickens. "*Los pollos killing los pollos*," we said. "I hated wringing and plucking and cutting up chickens from morning to night," he told me. "You couldn't breathe with the heat and all the feathers flying around. We were supposed to wear white masks over our noses and mouths, but it was so hot we couldn't bear them. We breathed feathers and chicken shit all day long, but I made out good, good enough to buy real papers, good enough to get a real job."

It is entirely possible to live in Salt Lake City and only speak Spanish. There are Josés in every restaurant, grocery store and hotel. Josés are roofing our houses, weeding our gardens, cleaning our kitchens. They move in for a while. They work. They send money home. They play soccer and volleyball in the parks on Sunday. In the bright light, we barely see them, never know them. And then they are gone.

The Great Basin is being inextricably pulled apart by tectonic forces. The distance between Salt Lake City and Los Angeles grows every year. Every time I think about this, I envision the earth silently ripping, a small tear forming along parched skin, while those of us standing on the edge slip down and under.

Winter arrived with its dry cold, and the sun still shone—harsh and blinding—as it often does in Utah. José didn't come anymore. I finished my novel, and it was published. And still I think of him. Did he finally buy that car he wanted, the one with shiny hubcaps? Or did I make that up? Did we ever speak of cars, or did I put those thoughts into Mario and then transfer them back onto José? I believe we spoke of horsemeat in Chiapas and the cold one would feel twenty kilometers outside Ocosingo. But did we? Today, I am unsure. Why can't I remember his real name, and where did he go?

José is present in the way that certain people come to inhabit our lives. Catchments. Mirrors. Mirages. Spaces we seek out, visit and return to in our continuous need to collect stories. Spaces that last for as long as they do, and then, with the shift in the season, they suddenly change form, like water vapor pulled into the shimmering Utah sky. Stories, absorbed into our minds, that become companions to our often-lonely lives.

Chapter 12

FINDING THE SLOW LANE

by Joni Haws

It's Radley's turn to pick the movie. I flip through the case and read him the choices. He picks *Diary of a Wimpy Kid*, again. Third-grade boys can't get enough of jokes involving moldy cheese. The trek from my parents' house in Hyrum to our home in South Jordan is conveniently movie-length. Teia immediately kicks off her shoes in the back seat.

"Click," Eden says, letting me know she is buckled in before we pull out. We wave to my mom as she stands in the doorway and then closes the door, no doubt to put away the leftover cake that neither of my parents are supposed to eat. I'll probably find it in the freezer next time I'm here. I put the car in gear, and we're on our way, taking the road past my old sledding hill and out around the reservoir. Just before reaching the canyon, the pavement rises and falls in a series of undulations that give tummies a good tickle. My kids raise their arms and pretend they're on a roller coaster.

It's mid-October, and we're too late to see the stunning mosaics of reds and golds that cloak the canyon in the fall. The transformation, now prime in the valleys, peaks earlier in the high elevations, and while a few tenacious patches remain, most of the trees have shivered down to bones. If only Dad had been born a couple of weeks earlier, we could have seen them.

We pass the entrance to Sherwood Hills, the hotel in the mountains where I worked in college washing the sheets and towels of people having more fun than I was having. Weeknights, when I worked my shift alone, I listened to my Discman and sang out loud, plowing my way through the endless bags of white linens. Weekends were busier. With the winter sun a harsh white

Joni Haws's kids. *Photo credit Joni Haws.*

behind the foggy windows, my coworker Debbie pulled out a stained sheet one Saturday morning and made a face.

"I'm never sleeping in a hotel bed again," she said, her voice glazed with laughter.

"I think that came from the Cadillac room. Probably a honeymoon," I said.

She saturated it with the watered-down Soft Scrub we used for bleach and shoved it in the giant chrome barrel of the washer, then unbuttoned the sleeves of her blue flannel shirt and pushed them up her arms. "I don't remember my honeymoon being so violent," she said.

I bit my lip, wondering if I should venture. It had taken me weeks to realize that the girlfriend she always talked about wasn't just a really supportive gal-pal. Turning the great knob to the on position, I asked, "How would you know?"

She grinned. "Yeah, wish I would have owned up to that before I married my ex-husband."

We worked in silence for a while, trading sheet corners and watching the stacks grow. The thrum of the machines vibrated through the concrete floor, the weight of so many towels bumping through each rotation of the dryer.

"I don't think things are going to work out with John," I told her.

Her penciled brows leapt. "What? I thought you said things were going really well."

"They were."

She shelved a stack of sheets and pulled her obsidian hair over one shoulder, combing through it with her fingers. "What happened?"

I sighed, already feeling the prickle of tears. "I don't know. He's great. He even drove all the way to my house from Brigham to give me a blessing when I was puking my guts out."

"That's a Mormon thing, right?" she asked.

"Yeah. Anyway, he's really sweet, killer smile, returned missionary. He sings and acts. It felt like everything was pulling us together, you know?" I paused, thinking of his intrepid kisses, somehow too technical, and that horrid Brazilian soccer shirt he wore everywhere. How that smile felt like a barrier I couldn't quite breach. "Why can't I make it feel right?" The tears spilled then.

Debbie clucked and wrapped an arm around my waist. "Sweetie, if he's not doing it for you, move on. You're what, twenty? You haven't even met half the men you're going to dump. You're just getting started."

I couldn't laugh. "I don't want to be just getting started." I thought of the stack of wedding announcements piling up beside my scrapbook at home. Those friends were starting their forevers. The thought of navigating another series of breakups made my chest ache. I pulled a washcloth from a dirty pile and wiped my nose with a corner.

The dryer blared, and Debbie pulled the warm towels onto the table. "Listen, hon, why don't you come to our house tonight? Me and Buzz are going to have a few beers and smoke a bowl. Just come hang out." She glanced at me through her lashes. "I'm worried about you."

Something broken stirred at her seemingly maternal plea, and it cut.

I almost went.

I crest the highest point of the canyon and start riding the brake, gripping the wheel at ten and two and scanning the hills for deer. The speed-trap cop seems to be off duty today, but I stay well below the speed limit, just in case. The kids are laughing at Greg and Rowley.

We round the last bend of the canyon, revealing the first of several temples strung like pearls along the collar of the Wasatch Mountains. I drive by the street that leads to John's old house without turning my head.

We turn south at the freeway. Eden is thirsty, and I hand her the full Camelbak, congratulating myself for my prescience. I drop the visor to combat the slumping sun and settle in, letting the mountains escort us home. My phone chimes, a text message. "Who's that from?" Teia asks. She must always know who it's from. "Dad," I tell her, "but I can't read it while I'm driving. I need to keep my eyes on the road." I hold my phone behind my head, waiting for it to be taken. She starts to giggle. "'When will you be home? You have a cute bum,'" she reads, choking on the words. I roll my eyes, but I'm smiling. "Tell him 6:30 and ask him if I should pick up McDonald's."

A thick, black jet thunders above us, landing at Hill Air Force Base. The kids are appropriately awed. I glimpse the Common Cents gas station where Royce and I got fountain drinks and candy bars a few years back, a simple moment made memorable by its rarity. Thirty years old, and I fell right back into baby sister mode. I still felt like the eight-year-old kid watching *Iron Eagle* with him in the basement.

"Why do they call it a dogfight?" I had asked.

"Because you're trying to bite the other plane without getting bit," he said, his animated face awash with freckles and a few pimples. He chewed beef jerky and leaned forward on the couch, his arms on his knees. I leaned too, empty-handed.

"What's that thing on his face?" I might have been exceeding the conversation-to-viewing ratio, but it was a very boring movie.

"It's supplying oxygen to the pilot in case the cockpit loses pressurization. It also helps him so he doesn't pass out. You can get up to eight or nine Gs on some of those turns!" He stared at me, so I tried to look impressed, though I wasn't confident he hadn't made up some of those words just to test my intelligence. The boy in the movie was cool by virtue of his Walkman and sleeveless sweatshirt, but the thought of Royce up in one of those

Joni Haws with her brothers. *Photo credit Joni Haws.*

jets scared me. I'd heard him saying something about an ROTC after his mission. I didn't know what that was.

"I can do a push-up," I told him.

"Oh yeah, let's see it!" The words dangled like catnip on a string, and I planted the toes of my multicolored high-tops on the carpet. Before I was halfway through the extension, his hand was on my back, pushing it down.

"It doesn't count if your butt's in the air. You gotta keep your back straight." I thought it *was* straight. My arms wobbled and then buckled, so I sat cross-legged on the floor while he executed twenty straight-back push-ups and then tossed me a smug smile. He flopped back onto the couch. "If you're gonna watch, watch."

I climbed up next to him, tucking my legs up to my chest. I wished I had some beef jerky.

"Look, it's the 'Goon,'" Eden shouts, referencing Lagoon, the only amusement park in the area, but I don't correct her. We spend the next several minutes listing as many rides as we can remember and counting up the months until next summer. Radley announces he needs to use the bathroom, and I ask him if he can hold it thirty more minutes. "Maybe," he says. I ask him if he went at Grandma's like I'd told him to. He doesn't remember. "I believe in you," I say.

The tall buildings of downtown Salt Lake huddle together like they're trying to keep warm. I don't blame them. The peaks behind them are already crowned white, and the bite in the air is only a hint of things to come.

"Is that the Salt Lake Temple?" Teia asks. Yes, I tell her. "Can we go see the lights at Christmas?"

"Ooh, yeah!" Radley seconds.

I say we'll see, but I already know I'll find an excuse to avoid it. The guilt niggles a bit, but there is little that can entice me to wander for hours in the cold anymore, even the millions of harlequin lights that adorn the trees at Temple Square.

I slip into the HOV lane as the traffic slows. My right leg is begging for a stretch, and McDonald's is actually starting to sound good. The Beastie Boys are singing "Intergalactic," so I know the movie has reached the school dance scene. It's almost over. I point to a tall building on our left and ask Eden if she knows what it is. Either she has truly forgotten since the last time I asked, or she just likes to act out the script, and she says no. "That's the hospital where you were born," I tell her. Teia offers up the next line: "Nine pounds, six ounces!" The numbers don't impress Eden, so I say, "Yup, my beautiful beefcake baby." She's grinning when I glance at her through the rearview mirror.

At the bottom of the valley, we point ourselves toward the copper mine, a series of massive, striated chocolate fountains where a mountain should be. I put my hand up to shield my eyes from the sun balancing on the rim of the Oquirrhs. We're minutes from home, but my mind is already there. I need to wash a load of whites so the boys will have shirts to wear to church in the morning, and I should really try to get some of the leaves raked up before it's completely dark. Teia folds the screen back into its niche in the ceiling when the movie ends.

Daren, dressed in jeans and a hoodie, is taking trash to the can as we pull into the driveway. I remind the kids to please wait until the car has stopped before opening the doors. Teia and Eden swarm him before I'm even out of the car, talking over each other. Radley shoots into the house, holding his pants.

Joni Haws with her husband and children. *Photo credit Joni Haws.*

"Hi," Daren says, trying to hug me with Eden between us clinging to his leg.

I hand him my purse while grabbing the bags of food from the passenger seat. "How'd it go today?" I ask.

"Good. I got a lot done," he says. I step into the house to find stacks of brown boxes, their seams slick with packing tape. Some are labeled "storage," some "apt."

"Did your dad feel bad that I wasn't there?" he asks as he rips the paper from a straw. The girls are already at the table diving into bags.

"I don't think so. I showed him the floorplan for the new house. I told him they can stay with us next Christmas." I take a sip of my Coke.

With the kids occupied, Daren steps close and puts his arms around me properly. His eyes are cradled in creases that deepen each year. "Want to get a Redbox?" he asks, squeezing my cute bum on the sly.

"There's a ton to do," I say.

"Yeah," is all he says.

It's quiet for a few seconds. They seem long. Through the window, I can see Sister Hurd bringing bags in from her car. Darkness is flirting.

"Yes, let's do get a Redbox," I say and head upstairs to exchange my shoes for slippers. "Nothing with fighting in it," I shout down. Leaves and laundry can wait. Tomorrow will find me just fine.

Chapter 13

SOME LINES ON FAULTS: AN INSOMNIAC'S DIARY

by Lynn Kilpatrick

Two Things that Keep Me Awake

Some days, I feel that my world will come crashing to an end when the Big Earthquake hits Salt Lake City. I live just above the East Bench Fault, and my house is made of brick. I also often imagine the Earth running out of water and all of us slowly dying of dehydration until the nightmare suburban landscape is littered with our desiccated corpses. These thoughts keep me awake at night. I feel like I'm living out a slight variation of the Robert Frost poem "Fire and Ice." He believed those were our only two options for human extinction: fire or ice. Now, of course, we know that there are endless varieties of ways we might wipe ourselves out: viral epidemic, buried alive under our own garbage, meteor (just like the dinosaurs). I know, however, that humans will die one of two ways: earthquake or drought. The drought option is particularly harrowing for me, as I have a fear of dehydration on an almost cellular level. I don't want to die by dehydration.

The Earth Might Swallow Me Up

Every year, my son participates in First Lego League, in which they are given a challenge, create a solution and then devise creative ways to present their solution. They also build and program Lego robots that enact certain aspects of the challenge theme. The challenges are problems like food storage, our

Utah Reflections

Fire and ice meet as the stars rain down on the snowy mountains. *Photo credit Jason Chacon.*

aging population, natural disasters. The annual competition, where the robots engage in thematic missions on a playing board with miniature Lego obstacles and the teams present their creative solutions, is held at a local elementary school. Each team displays their projects on tri-fold boards that depict the year's theme with their solutions. This year the theme was Nature's Fury. Walking through these colorfully illustrated displays was like taking a tour of my own nightmares. One board displayed photographs of recent earthquakes, roads buckled, houses disintegrated as if they were made of sand. These are the images that populate my pre-sleep brain. I picture my own house, a pile of bricks, me, trapped somewhere inside it, and the hole that would obviously appear in the road to consume my car, the pavement, large trees. The only thought that gives me comfort when I imagine this earthquake scenario is that the man who lives across the street has done all the emergency training, and if I were lying in the rubble of my house, I'm certain he would look for me. When the earthquake hits Salt Lake City, I sometimes think as I lay awake at night, at least someone will find my body.

STORIES FROM THE WASATCH FRONT

But Then Again...Water...

I'm not sure why I have such a fear of dehydration, but I attach some importance to a childhood incident that occurred in Phoenix. My grandparents lived in Phoenix, and for some reason, we visited them during the summer. We were at a flea market when I felt like I might faint and/or die. I remember going back to my grandparents' car and sitting in the front seat, directly in front of the air conditioner. I don't remember drinking water, though I must have. Ever since then, even when I lived in Seattle where it rains every day, I have never left the house without water. I always have my trusty water bottle, even when I have to fly somewhere. I bring it empty to the airport, and then as soon as I'm through security, I find a water fountain and fill it up. My water bottle is a liquid-containing security blanket. I'm sure that even if I die of natural causes, I will be found clutching my water bottle. Of all the nightmare humanity-destroying scenarios I have imagined, dying of dehydration seems by far the worst fate. I imagine the way our skin would cling to our bones, like tissues catching on a fence. Perhaps it is because great expanses of the West are desert, but dehydration seems like a perfectly rational fear. If I ever prayed, or if I had a mantra, it would probably be something like *Not dehydration. Please.*

The Big One

In spite of the fact that I'm fairly certain I will die of dehydration, I spend a fair amount of time trying to reconcile myself with the fact that, eventually, there will be an earthquake in Salt Lake City. At the Utah Museum of Natural History, there are several hands-on exhibits that allow visitors to create models of various size earthquakes. One exhibit that I go back to again and again is a model that simulates what happens to buildings when earthquakes hit. You can build structures of various heights made of different materials and then choose an earthquake from the past to see how your structure would fare. What this game teaches me is that we have no idea how to deal with earthquakes. The quake in this exhibit is simulated using a flat piece of wood that shakes with various degrees of intensity. Perhaps it would be too upsetting to children if the base simply buckled in two and the structure collapsed, no matter how flexible its beams. There are no sexy survival scenarios with earthquakes. I remember the earthquake in 1989 when a bridge outside Oakland collapsed. The

Utah Reflections

Clouds sit heavy on the Wasatch Front, ready to drop snow. *Photo credit Jason Chacon.*

photographs of the gaping maw of metal kept me awake for days. Every time I think about earthquakes, I become more and more convinced that this is how the entire human population will be destroyed. But with an earthquake, maybe our deaths would be quick; we might simply be crushed in the jaws of the Earth itself.

Not a Drop to Drink

Dehydration seems so cruel. In the demented hypotheses of my mind, humans would become dried out, like organic apricots. Saying that now, I feel some sympathy for the apricots and plums that undergo a long session of baking in special machines to transform them from voluptuous to chewy. I don't like to imagine myself as leather, but perhaps it is useful to do so. In exercises of mental fortitude, the important step is to rob your fear of its power over you. If I imagine myself emaciated and dry, reduced to just my skin, perhaps I will no longer fear it. But this supposition is fundamentally wrong. The more I imagine myself as skin sack, devoid of water, the more I fear dehydration. The only thing that keeps me from screaming is to pour myself a tall drink of water and then to drink it. The rush of liquid into my body is akin to taking a long, deep breath. Why are we so cavalier in our day-to-day interactions with water? If recent events concerning municipal drinking water are any indication, though, my fears may be misplaced. As humans, we are probably more likely to poison or pollute our water than to run out of it completely. We'll have plenty of it, but we won't be able to drink it. *Water, water, everywhere...*

Either Way...

Perhaps all these thoughts and nightmare scenarios are just a way to rehearse the inevitable death that we all know is coming. Yes, we will all die. Okay. But we can't know how. Every day, someone dies in a totally ridiculous and avoidable way. One man was attacked by a beaver. Another by choking on a cockroach that he had eaten voluntarily. One guy was crushed by a bale of hay. I'm sure all of these will become scenes in future nightmares that I am already planning on having. It will be hard to take the beaver seriously, though, even if their teeth are totally ferocious. Maybe in the dream, my

The Wasatch Mountains hold the summer's water on their shoulders. *Photo credit Jason Chacon.*

brain will soften the danger of the attack by giving the animal soft, cuddly-looking fur. And perhaps this is the way we deal with our fears, by softening them somehow, by making them less awful than they really would be. So I tell myself that the earthquake wouldn't be quite so bad, because my neighbor would find me (or at least my body). Dying of thirst wouldn't be so bad because…well, that one's harder. Luckily, one of the symptoms of dehydration is the inability to think clearly, so hopefully I would just hallucinate that I was in a giant pool, and then as my brain began to shrink up like a cauliflower in the desert, I would relive the sensation of all those tall glasses of water. Maybe I would imagine I was drowning in a deep, cold lake. Perhaps my brain would be so fractured that I wouldn't even notice I was dying. Perhaps the real nightmare scenario, one my brain is working on the details of right now, is one wherein the Earth suffers a series of catastrophic earthquakes, beginning right here in Salt Lake, with a giant schism in the East Bench Fault the aftershocks of which cause earthquakes in California and Australia and Chile. As a result of all this tectonic shifting, all the fresh water from the mountains will drain away, right down into the core of the Earth, so that humanity will be destroyed by earthquakes *and* dehydration. I'm fairly certain that is how it will happen.

Chapter 14

HOLD THIS

by Kase Johnstun

I stood outside the old 1956 Willies Jeep and looked up at the tall bench seat in front of me. My dad circled around the front of the Jeep and opened the driver's side door. He looked down at me through the emptiness in the cab of the truck and stood there drinking his coffee with his rifle slung over his back. His thick, blond hair shot straight out of the side of his cap.

"Well, get in," my uncle Randy, who stood next to my dad, said to me. He placed his hand on my back, a small form of encouragement from a man I looked up to, literally and metaphorically. My breath turned to steam when it left my mouth and touched the cold Utah morning air. My tiny hand reached to grab the little metal handle of the interior doorframe of the old Jeep, the exposed frame of the thick metal strong enough to withstand a rollover but porous enough to let in the cold wind of late fall.

I pulled myself up and moved immediately to the center of the cab, and my legs straddled the long stick shift that seemed to come three feet off the floor. Its long black neck showed the age of the old climber. Deep nicks revealed years of use and the durability of vehicle construction in the mid-twentieth century. I felt the springs of the old seat beneath me. A thin, braided, blue-, yellow- and white-striped seat cover blanketed the seat that was made up of springs and metal framing. Each shift of my butt found a damaged spring that pinched my ass, but I didn't complain.

My dad climbed into the driver's seat next to me. His six-foot, boxy frame consumed the woven seat beneath him. His elbow sat nearly on top of my

Utah Reflections

The drastic slants of Snowbasin wait to be climbed. *Photo credit Jason Chacon.*

tiny shoulder but not quite. It anchored me into the threaded seat just firmly enough to hold me in place. Bumpy, dirt roads were coming our way.

My uncle Randy reached into the cab with his rifle slung around his narrow but strong shoulders and extended a green thermos and an empty coffee cup toward me.

"Hold this," he said to me. In my family growing up, the men never asked their boys to do something; they told them to do something. They demanded with a firmness that said in two little words: hold this, don't drop it and do not ask if you can give it back before I ask for it back; got it?

After handing me the coffee, he pulled the rifle off his shoulder, put it carefully into its carrier and tucked it behind the long bench seat of the cab. He sat next to me on my right, leaning onto the door, shuffling to get comfortable. He rolled down the window and draped his arm out the car door because it was going to be cold until we got the heater cranked up, and he might as well be comfortable in the cold.

"Hand me those," he said to me. He grabbed the thermos from my hands, twisted the lid off the top and filled his cup with coffee. The steam from the top of the thermos filled the yet unheated cab, and the smell of it weaved its way into my nostrils. The smell saturated my memories. It dug deep into places in my mind that it would never leave, places that held on to moments like these, places that will never let go of the deep, rich coffee smell of that morning, the rich, thick warmth of steam that mixed with the cold, dry air.

"Doyle?" My uncle Randy extended the thermos.

"Yes, sir," my dad responded to his longtime friend. My uncle filled my dad's mug and handed it back to him. My dad immediately handed the mug to me.

"Hold this," he said. I slid the fingers of my right hand into the mug handle and then wrapped my left hand around the other side of the mug. I held it as tightly as I could. My cloth gloves didn't provide the firm grip I had hoped to have when holding such a valuable item. The warmth penetrated my gloves and shot straight up my arm to my heart.

It's funny. I had to be about six or seven. I can't say for sure. But, looking back, it is one of my first deep, clear memories of being alone with the men of the family, one of the first full-sensory memories without women. If I were seven, my dad and my uncle would have been in their mid-thirties. I am in my mid-thirties as I write this. But I see them as they are now. They are not thirty-four-year-old young men in my memory. They don't seem as immature as I feel. My uncle has gray hair with glasses, and his face is leathery from forty years of sitting in the sun in a tall crane, erecting giant buildings to change the cityscape of Salt Lake City, Kansas City or Pittsburgh. I see my dad as he is now. He is a sixty-year-old man, heavy-set with deep smile lines that depart from the edge of his lips and gray hair that streaks though his blond head. I don't see the young men they were. I can't imagine their minds filled with the insecurities that swim through mine daily. I can't envision them still making stupid mistakes. I can't see them as my age when I feel so short in the tooth at thirty-eight years old.

My dad turned the key to get the old Jeep started. It started with a boom, not with the single rev of my little Hyundai that sits outside, but with a boom that broke the morning quiet. He shoved the stick into first and then pushed down the spatula-sized clutch, a clutch with no padding or emblems, just metal and porous.

"Hold this." My dad put the stick into my hands to hold in first gear. He kept a foot on the clutch and one on the brake and arranged his gun behind the seat. I quickly took my left hand off the coffee mug and wrapped it as tightly as I could around the giant stick shift. It rumbled in my grasp. I held two very important things: the stick to make the car go in the morning and the coffee to make my dad go in the morning. I pushed with everything I could toward first gear and squeezed the mug with my slippery, gloved hand.

He probably only fiddled with his bag for ten seconds, but by the time he returned his hand to the clutch, my arm felt as if it were going to give. He sat down quickly. He turned up the heat. He grabbed his cup of coffee. He took a sip. He gave it back to me.

"Hold this," he said. We held a lot of things for them back then—wrenches, screwdrivers, rifles, knives, deer entrails, fish. That morning before a hunt, I held coffee mugs and stick shifts.

My dad placed his hand on my knee and looked down at me. His eyes looked directly into mine as they always have. He is not a man who looks away. He looks you directly in the eye and expects the same of you.

"Ready to go, bud?" he asked.

I looked up to my right and saw my uncle Randy looking down at me. His face asked the same question—*ready to go, bud?* I looked back up to my dad. With both doors finally shut, with the heater finally kicked on, with the coffee cup in my hand and with the deepest smell of coffee surrounding us, I felt ready. I sat squished between two grown men, but I couldn't have been more comfortable and happy.

For some reason, my brother and cousin didn't join us that morning, and my grandpa passed on the trip. I really don't care to find out why, but it was just the three of us, and I think of it every time I smell coffee and feel the crisp air of the cold fall.

"Yeah," I said, looking back and forth at both of them. "Yeah, I'm ready."

Chapter 15
INTIMATIONS OF VITALITY: CLIMBING LITTLE COTTONWOOD

by Jeffrey McCarthy

The ingredients are natural: granite, sky, the ribbled trunk of a fir tree incongruously thriving at this height. And fear. Yes, fear is natural, too, for the climber on the climb. It is, in a sense, the goal, as drunk is the goal of drink. Not too much fear, mind you, but just enough. There are places on these granite heights where a little slip will start a big fall and someone's brother, someone's son, in that moment becomes gravity's orphan. What's wanted is sufficient fear to focus the thoughts, to harden the grip, to remind us each of our better selves here in Little Cottonwood Canyon. I know people who moved to Utah for this granite and others who set their schedules by its moods. The climbs here come in all sizes—long, foot-intensive pads up the featureless slabs; steep cracks that are all edges and holds but stern in their angle; and wandering, daylong routes that connect feature to feature and offer varied tests and pleasures. This vertical context challenges me with the thought that being human is being part of the physical world that touches me while I touch it.

From the first belay, the crack you want is well to the right, but to get there, you start left to gain a horizontal flake that you don't grab so much as squeeze, like an old acquaintance at a party. With this firm embrace, the feet can go right and the hands stay engaged, a personal balance between self and stone that passes eerily above belayer and belay to reach, soon, the thin crack and the new challenge of balance to come.

Utah Reflections

The granite here is affable—shallow dishes for the feet, distinct edges on the hands—it's as consistent and reliable as any relative. Unlike, say, limestone, who offsets the joy of featuredness with the sin of looseness. Granite is the old friend who might test you but will never betray you.

On this climb, the next stage is tricky because it's hard to protect. The footholds narrow, the hands lose authority. One steps up into a shallow vertical scoop and gains balance there to look up and see a loving, inviting hand crack…but it's ten feet away. Between here and there, only the subtle foot placements on awkward curving stone complemented by what balance the hands can find. Here the granite tests the body that in other spots it embraced. The gear is a tiny metal wedge pressed hopefully into a broken gap, and the stone leans toward you, expectant but now unhelpful.

The feet move up first, hunching the body into an un-balance rectifiable only by ascent. Sometimes the body rebels, but on better days, it thanks the feet and stretches upward, optimistic the hands will find new balance and the shoes will keep their grip. That accomplished, the feet must come up again and again smear hopefully in awkward scallops, and now the protection feels far away, but the climber is too uneasy to go back down and the body must do what the mind resists and stretch again upward. Here the stone assists, and while a foot begins perhaps to slide, one hand finds a bit more purchase at its very height, and the granite there is an ally, and the urge to rise toward that friendship, the incut crack whispering "welcome," that urge swings the other hand from its nebulous pressing up, up and into the doughty handclasp of reliable granite, and from there a yet firmer grip appears and the feet find new balance and the world appears around you with its clouds and birds and green, green trees. Below, Little Cottonwood Creek sings its song to the breeze and the day marches on.

To climb a route several times is to build a relationship with the stone. I can't count the times I've made these moves, known this anticipation, felt the stone encourage me and then hold me in that sweet grasp. Is it six times? Is it ten? No matter; the point is that in Little Cottonwood, one returns to the great climbs, and in doing so, the little human gains a certain brightness, a lamp to shine into the shadows of our relation with the natural world. Those gray granite walls are a stern arena to rebuke the feckless and reward the careful, but beyond these mere physical entanglements, they counsel those who can hear and feel that stone's

Jeff McCarthy cresting a rock. *Photo credit Jeff McCarthy*.

accent. You see, we think of rock as inert, and we think of nature as a passive object for our active, instrumental selves. But in coming back to climbs, we find the stone in new moods and ourselves in small communion with those grand presences.

The experience of climbing routes again and again reemphasizes moments of insight about human relations to the natural world. In particular, I linger on the transition from uncertainty to traction—almost falling becomes the hand engulfed by solid stone and then transcending, as though some strong friend reached down to pull you up onto a dock. The climbers fortunate enough to know Little Cottonwood season after season likewise come to know their physical selves in a reciprocal relation to the active presence, the fleshly claims of the non-human world around them.

Afternoon becomes evening, and I descend on a doubled rope, the strands warm from friction, moving through space, my mind conscious of the rope's bobbing ends, my feet walking their own walk down the granite's most welcoming angles. Part of the rappel takes me past the crack I've climbed, and in its chalky edges, I see the record of my own passage and, just maybe, an intimation of vitality. This canyon granite touches us back. It offers more than a passive setting for play; these steeps open body and mind to the vibrant presence of an active nature. When I'm coiling that rope at the base, there's a hush that surrounds me, and I find that if I'm very quiet, I can hear these walls humming the song of the earth.

Chapter 16
THEN CAME NOVEMBER

by Chadd VanZanten

Let me explain the way winter arrives here at the northern tip of the Wasatch. Because you might be under the impression it arrives at the Winter Solstice, December 21 or thereabouts, the same as in other places. You may think it has something to do with the declination of the sun—the way it rides so low in the sky and sets before ever chasing the icy sparkle from the banked-up snow.

You'd be wrong about that.

Around here, winter begins in December, but it arrives much earlier. It may come as early as Labor Day. It might hold off until Thanksgiving. Most typically, it's October.

It happens like this. You hike up a hollow in Blacksmith Fork Canyon to fly-fish an isolated stretch of that river. The maple leaves are blood-red and the aspens are golden, but at noon you'd swear it's still August. So, you're wearing a T-shirt. There are nine different flies pinned to your cap, but you've not decided which to tie on yet because the fish you're after haven't exhibited the faintest sign of choosiness for several months. They'll bite down on almost anything.

Then you notice the absence of grasshoppers fleeing through the dry grass at your feet, and just as you're about to bring this to the attention of your fishing buddy, a gray, wet cloud slides across the sun, and instead you ask him, "Hey, did you bring a jacket?"

"No," he says, face upturned. "Did you?"

"I didn't."

Utah Reflections

Photo of the beautiful Cache Valley snowy riverbank. *Photo credit Chadd VanZanten.*

It gets cold in a hurry, but you fish anyway. The wind blows and there's rain. Hands get so raw and pruned you start trying to remember where you left your winter gloves. Somewhere in your truck, hopefully. You catch fewer fish than you caught a week ago. Fewer by half. That's because you're fishing as if it's summer. But it's not. Winter has arrived. It hasn't started yet, but it has come.

This year, winter hit me like a delivery van. The last thing I remember distinctly is a trip to the outer Cub River. Mid-October. The water was clear as gin, and a rust-colored caddis fly worked all day like a voodoo fetish to coax almost fifty cutthroat trout to my net.

Those cutthroats were reckless. They came up from deep holes, crossed from one side of the channel to the other to take a fly. They came up two at a time. Those fish were irrational. I was extra careful when returning each to the stream that day. Clearly, they could not be trusted with their own safety.

After the sun ducked behind the limestone rim of the canyon, the fishing cooled off. I sat down to remove a pebble from my boot. I had been walking on it for hours, thinking if I stopped even for a minute to take it out, I might break the spell. That was the last in a string of such days.

Stories from the Wasatch Front

The wide river view that cuts the Cache Valley. *Photo credit Chadd VanZanten.*

Then came November, and there he was. Winter. Unmistakably.

A temperature inversion, a mass of frigid, immoveable air, settled into the valley, trapping beneath it a dirty mist of ice and automobile exhaust. The sun shone whitely through the haze like a portal to some paler, colder universe.

For a week solid, it never got above twenty degrees. The fog grew so dense that the Wellsville Mountains, which rise like a fortress wall at the western edge of the valley, were obscured from view for days, glimpsed only at evening against the violet pollution of sundown.

Anchor ice began appearing on the floor of the Logan River. The small tributary streams like Rock Creek and Right Hand Fork were already frozen over. At Merlin Olsen Park, in the neighborhood they call the Island, the city workers got out the firehoses at night and started laying down the ice-skating rink, a ritual that typically doesn't commence until after the holidays are completely done.

It wasn't even December yet.

When the days grow so short and dim, everything seems more serious than it actually is. A summertime problem is a wintertime crisis. A crisis

Utah Reflections

The beautiful Cache Valley with mountains in the distance. *Photo credit Chadd VanZanten.*

in autumn becomes a calamity just a month or two later. If I tell you I was struggling with a major personal emergency in early November, that should indicate my condition on the first weekend in December, which is when it got even colder. Single-digit temperatures during the day and below zero all night.

Such extremes are not unknown here. There is a place in Logan Canyon where the temperature may dip to sixty degrees below zero. But that's only in the dead cold of January and at an elevation of 8,100 feet. I was wallowing down on the valley floor, and the Winter Solstice was still two weeks away.

Ordinarily, I wouldn't fish in weather like that, and my autumn crisis made me want to fish even less. But I'd made arrangements to fish with my friend Littrell, who was visiting from Texas. Littrell had never fished this part of the country, and although he was here on business and staying for only a few days, he'd gotten it into his head that he must catch a trout from one of our high mountain streams.

I advised against this.

"You understand how cold it is out there," I said.

"Yes."

"You understand there's a decent chance we may perish," I said.

"I'd still like to give it a try."

On the morning of December 7, the temperature stood at five degrees. The inversion was gone, but the wind gusted to twenty knots. Factoring windchill, it was seventeen below zero at the Spring Hollow Bridge, which is where we stepped lightly over the bankside shelves of ice and lowered ourselves into the Logan River.

We fished. I number that day among the worst I've ever known. After each cast, the water froze onto the actual flyline, forming a glassy chain that could be cleared off only with considerable effort. It's a phenomenon I'd never experienced. Between that and the down-canyon wind, it was difficult even to cast in a forward direction, and accuracy was out of the question. My waders, too, were laminated in ice, and hoarfrost formed on my beard.

After twenty minutes, Littrell shouted, "I can't cast. Everything's frozen up."

I shouldered my rod and slogged across the stream to him. Windblown spray stung my face and froze on my glasses. I steered Littrell toward the one promising riverbend I thought we might prospect before succumbing to exposure.

"Cast in there," I said, pointing, voice raised against the wind. "Cast right in there."

Littrell's ice-hampered fly line flopped over heavily and nowhere in the vicinity I'd indicated.

"There?" he asked.

"If that is the best you can do, then, yes. There."

Logan, Cache Valley, with mountains and the LDS Temple among the reds and oranges of late fall. *Photo credit Danel W. Bachman.*

Utah Reflections

By some accident, Littrell's fly slid through the bend, and he set his hook on a small brown trout. I took a photo as evidence that it had happened. It was hard to know if that fish even wanted to get back in the water. Within ten minutes, we had retreated to our trucks, and we have not spoken of the matter since.

My troubles worsened. I lost track of what day it was, forgot appointments. I slept a lot. My family asked me what was wrong. I refused to explain myself. Friends told me they were worried. I claimed to be fine. My plan was to fish through it all, to take my problems into the mountains and lay them there like some melancholy and reticent hero. This didn't really work. Winter had pushed me to the ground, and I guess he stood with his foot on my neck awhile because I couldn't take a clean, deep breath for a month.

But there's something else that happens in wintertime around here. Every so often, there is a break in the weather. Despite my many years in the valley, I'd forgotten.

It happens like this. You go out to your truck carrying your fly rod and net, and although the garage is a mere thirty feet from the back door, you put on gloves and wrap a scarf over your face to prevent your nostrils from freezing shut. As you drive south through Nibley and Mendon, you hold one hand over the heater vent, then the other, wondering if you might reach the Blacksmith Fork before the truck even warms up.

Then you notice a rupture in the canopy of the inversion, out over the Wellsvilles, as if there were a weak spot in the sky there. You fumble for your sunglasses as the sun glares through the gloom. Soon, the haze overhead turns dark blue, and all around is melting, dripping.

This year, the break came when I met up with Jason one day to fish at the Oneida Narrows on the Bear River. It lies at the uppermost limits of the Wasatch, on the Idaho side. Jason brought his dog, a yellow lab that waits by the riverbank while we fish and then charges madly into the water to chase the fish we hook. We call her the Blonde Torpedo of Destiny.

It was the first time in a long time I'd fished the Bear. As we drove along the back roads through the old township site of Egypt and north through the pasturelands, I confessed I didn't know the best way to catch anything that day.

"We can swing some streamers," said Jason.

"Maybe try some nymphs," I replied.

When we stepped out of Jason's mud-sprayed Honda, we knew it was the kind of day when catching fish is less than paramount. The air was clear and windless, the sky an improbable cerulean.

It got warmer as we pulled on our waders and hiked a mile or so downstream. Everything was melting, dripping. The Blonde Torpedo loped out ahead through the snow, mouth agape, tongue lolling. A bald eagle coursed overhead so low I saw its eye winking like a camera shutter as it tilted its head to examine us.

We swung our streamers. We tried some nymphs. The fish obliged us.

I watched Jason hook a small rainbow trout. His dog splashed over to investigate as the fish was landed and let go again. I squinted into the glimmer of the sun on the water. Jason raised his face to the sky.

"This day," he said, shaking the water from his hand. "I mean, my God, what a day."

The Vernal Equinox would fall on the twentieth of March, then and always, here and everywhere. But in Cache Valley, spring had arrived. It hadn't started, but it had come.

ABOUT THE AUTHORS

STEVAN ALLRED is the author of *A Simplified Map of the Real World*, a collection of fifteen linked short stories set in the fictional town of Renata. His short stories, essays and poems have appeared in numerous literary journals and websites. His zine, *Dixon Ticonderoga*, explores the intimate connection between pencils and divorce. He teaches writing at the Pinewood Table in Portland, Oregon.

PHYLLIS BARBER is the author of eight books, including a memoir trilogy: *How I Got Cultured: A Nevada Memoir* (a coming-of-age story that won the Associated Writing Program Award for Creative Nonfiction in 1991 and the Association of Mormon Letters Award in Biography in 1993); *Raw Edges: A Coming-of-Age-in-Middle-Age Account*; and *To the*  *Mountain: One Mormon Woman's Search for Spirit*, due out from Quest Books in 2014. She is the mother of four sons, a founder of the Writers at Work Conference and a teacher in the Vermont College of Fine Arts MFA in Writing Program for many years.

About the Authors

KATHARINE COLES'S fifth poetry collection, *The Earth Is Not Flat* (Red Hen 2013), was written under the auspices of the National Science Foundation's Antarctic Artists and Writers Program; her sixth, *Flight*, will be out in 2016. Recent poems have appeared in *Poetry*, *The Seneca Review*, *Virginia Quarterly Review*, *Image* and other journals; recent nonfiction has been published in *Ascent* and *Crazyhorse*. A professor of English at the University of Utah, in 2009 and 2010 she served as the inaugural director of the Poetry Foundation's Harriet Monroe Poetry Institute. She received a Guggenheim Foundation Fellowship for 2012–13.

J. SCOTT HALE lives in Atlanta, Georgia, with his wife and three children. While growing up in Utah, Scott grew to love the outdoors and activities including fly-fishing, mountain biking and white-water rafting. Scott studied biology at the University of Utah and received a PhD in immunology from the University of Washington. He returns to Utah whenever he can to enjoy the mountains and rivers that he loves.

JONI HAWS is a native of Cache Valley, raised in Hyrum, where she learned the arts of snow removal and driving a manual transmission. After marrying her husband and living in sundry locations across the country, she has called the Salt Lake Valley home since 2008. She is a graduate of Utah State University with a degree in English literature and an active member of the Church of Jesus Christ of Latter-Day Saints. When she's not searching the house for the chronically missing shoes of her three children, she enjoys writing, crocheting, belting rock ballads and keeping library books just a little past their due dates. She can also be heard on the Mormon-themed podcast *The Cultural Hall*.

About the Authors

JEN HENDERSON grew up in Sunset, Utah, just a few miles from the Great Salt Lake. In 2000, she left the state for graduate school, though she imagines a time when she'll again enjoy the profile of the Wasatch Front from her front yard. Jen holds an MFA in creative nonfiction from Goucher College and is currently completing a PhD in science and technology studies at Virginia Tech. She lives in southwest Virginia with her husband, digital artist Dane Webster, and her four Appalachian-born felines. To learn more about her work, visit jenhenderson.com.

PAM HOUSTON's most recent book is *Contents May Have Shifted*, published in 2012. She is also the author of two collections of linked short stories, *Cowboys Are My Weakness* and *Waltzing the Cat: The Novel*; *Sight Hound*; and a collection of essays, *A Little More About Me*, all published by W.W. Norton. Her stories have been selected for volumes of Best American Short Stories, the O. Henry Awards, the 2013 Pushcart Prize and Best American Short Stories of the Century. She is the winner of the Western States Book Award, the WILLA award for contemporary fiction, the Evil Companions Literary Award and multiple teaching awards. She is a professor of English at UC–Davis, directs the literary nonprofit Writing by Writers and teaches in the Pacific University low-residency MFA program and at writers' conferences around the country and the world. She lives on a ranch at nine thousand feet in Colorado near the headwaters of the Rio Grande.

LYNN KILPATRICK's essays have appeared in *Creative Nonfiction*, *Ninth Letter* and *Brevity*. Her short story collection, *In the House*, was published by FC2. She earned a PhD from the University of Utah and teaches at Salt Lake Community College. She lives in Salt Lake City with her husband and son.

About the Authors

LANCE LARSEN, poet laureate of Utah, has published four poetry collections, most recently *Genius Loci* (Tampa, 2013). His prose appears widely, and two pieces have been listed as notable essays in Best American Essays 2005 and 2009. He has received a number of awards, including a Pushcart Prize and a fellowship from the National Endowment for the Arts. A professor at BYU, he has lived for the last twenty years in Springville with his wife, Jacqui Larsen, a mixed-media artist, and together they have directed several study abroad programs in London and Madrid.

JEFFREY MATHES MCCARTHY is director of the MA program in Environmental Humanities at the University of Utah. He has written extensively for academic journals and mountain magazines. His book *Contact: Mountain Climbing and Environmental Thinking* was published by the University of Nevada Press.

JANA RICHMAN is the author of a memoir, *Riding in the Shadows of Saints: A Woman's Story of Motorcycling the Mormon Trail*, and two novels, *The Last Cowgirl* and *The Ordinary Truth*. Jana was born and raised in Utah's west desert, the daughter of a small-time rancher and a hand-wringing Mormon mother. She writes about issues that threaten to destroy the essence of the West: overpopulation, overdevelopment, rapidly dwindling water aquifers, stupidity, ignorance, arrogance and greed. She also writes about passion, beauty and love. She lives in the small town of Escalante, Utah, bordering the Grand Staircase–Escalante National Monument, with her husband and backpacking partner, Steve Defa.

About the Authors

Sylvia Torti is a biologist and creative writer. Her first novel, *The Scorpion's Tail*, was published in 2005 and won the Miguel Mármol Award for "best debut fiction by an American of Latino/a descent." Her short stories and essays have been published in numerous magazines and edited volumes. She has just completed her second novel, *Birdsong*. Currently, she is dean of the Honors College at the University of Utah.

Chadd VanZanten's essays on fly-fishing appear in the online fly-fishing journal *Eat Sleep Fish*. His short fiction can be found in *The Provo Orem Word* and the prose and poetry collection *In the Shimmering* (LUW Press). Chadd lives in Logan, where he works as a professional editor. When he is not writing, he is fishing. The opposite is also true.

James R. West lived an active life in South Ogden until he joined the marines at eighteen. His dad taught him how to fish, hunt and help others. His mom taught him how to ice skate and play cards. At six, he was caught hitchhiking by the police. That same year, he made ten bucks selling his first-grade photos to neighbors. He once told his parents he was going to run away. To Ogden.

Terry Tempest Williams is the author of fourteen books, including *Refuge, Leap, The Open Space of Democracy, Finding Beauty in a Broken World* and, most recently, *When Women Were Birds*. She is currently the Annie Clark Tanner Scholar in Environmental Humanities at the University of Utah. Recipient of a John Simon Guggenheim Memorial Fellowship and a Lannan Literary Fellowship in nonfiction, she divides her time between Castle Valley, Utah, and Moose, Wyoming.

ABOUT THE EDITORS

SHERRI H. HOFFMAN is a working writer, sports fanatic and graphic designer. Some of her work has appeared in *December* magazine, *Etchings*, *PANK*, *Brave On the Page: Oregon Writers on Craft and the Creative Life* and various online publications. She is a Pushcart Prize nominee, recipient of the UWM Chancellor's Award, graduate of Weber State University and the 2013 MFA student commencement speaker at Pacific University, where she also received her MFA. Sherri is currently a fiction editor at *Cream City Review* and is teaching creative writing and working on a PhD in creative writing at the University of Wisconsin–Milwaukee. She loves birds, her family and a good cuppa coffee.

KASE JOHNSTUN is an award-winning essayist and author of *Release* (forthcoming from McFarland) whose work has appeared nationally and internationally in journals and magazines such as *Creative Nonfiction Magazine*, the *Chronicle Review*, *Label Me Latina/o*, *Prime Number* and the *Watershed Review* and as a regular contribution to *The Good Men Project*, as well as many other spots. He has an MA and an

About the Editors

MFA in creative writing, and recently, his set of essays *Tortillas for Honkies and "Other" Essays* (unpublished) was named a finalist for the Autumn House Press 2013 Award in Creative Nonfiction.

MARY VANLEEUWEN JOHNSTUN works as a technical writer and project director by day and writer by night. A Kansan by birth, Mary has lived along the Wasatch Front since 2001, when she jumped at the opportunity to take an internship at the University of Utah, trading rolling hills of wheat for brilliant mountains. Mary received her MA degree in English/culture studies from Kansas State University and is a proud resident of Ogden, Utah.

Visit us at
www.historypress.net

This title is also available as an e-book

www.ingramcontent.com/pod-product-compliance
Lightning Source LLC
Chambersburg PA
CBHW060812100426
42813CB00004B/1047